Lincoln before *Lincoln*

Lincoln BEFORE *Lincoln*

Early Cinematic Adaptations of the Life of America's Greatest President

BRIAN J. SNEE

Scholarly publisher for the Commonwealth,
serving Bellarmine University, Berea College, Centre College of Kentucky, Eastern Kentucky University, The Filson Historical Society, Georgetown College, Kentucky Historical Society, Kentucky State University, Morehead State University, Murray State University, Northern Kentucky University, Transylvania University, University of Kentucky, University of Louisville, and Western Kentucky University.

Editorial and Sales Offices: The University Press of Kentucky
663 South Limestone Street, Lexington, Kentucky 40508-4008
www.kentuckypress.com

Library of Congress Cataloging-in-Publication Data

Names: Snee, Brian J., author.
Title: Lincoln before Lincoln : early cinematic adaptations of the life of America's greatest president / Brian J. Snee.
Description: Lexington : The University Press of Kentucky, 2016. | Includes bibliographical references and index.
Identifiers: LCCN 2016000228| ISBN 9780813167473 (hardcover : alk. paper) | ISBN 9780813167497 (pdf) | ISBN 9780813167480 (epub)
Subjects: LCSH: Lincoln, Abraham, 1809–1865—In motion pictures.
Classification: LCC PN1995.9.L53 S65 2016 | DDC 791.43/651—dc23
LC record available at http://lccn.loc.gov/2016000228

This book is printed on acid-free paper meeting the requirements of the American National Standard for Permanence in Paper for Printed Library Materials.

Manufactured in the United States of America.

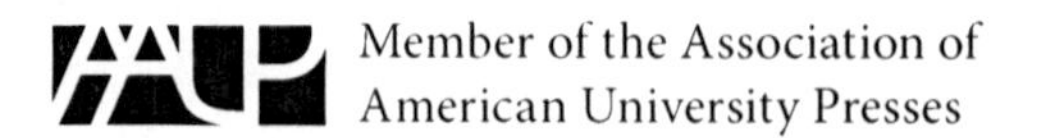

For Jackson & Bella
The better angels of my nature

Contents

Preface

Abraham Lincoln has had a long and mysterious history in Hollywood. The subject of tens of thousands of books, Lincoln would seem to be an obvious favorite for filmmakers. However, the list of major movies and television miniseries about Lincoln's life is surprisingly short. Countless films feature Lincoln cameos, such as the ubiquitous scene in which the president pardons a Civil War soldier sentenced to death either for desertion or falling asleep on duty. Yet only a few films have contributed substantially to Lincoln's place in American memory.

Given the recent and remarkable success of Stephen Spielberg's *Lincoln* (2012), it is entirely possible that that film will come to be regarded as the definitive cinematic portrait of Abraham Lincoln—the *reel* Lincoln that future generations will turn to when searching for the *real* Lincoln. If that is true, it is all the more vital that we now ask: How has Hollywood represented Lincoln before *Lincoln?* This book examines closely several movies and miniseries that preceded and likely influenced Spielberg's film: *The Birth of a Nation* (1915), *Abraham Lincoln* (1930), *Young Mr. Lincoln* (1939), *Abe Lincoln in Illinois* (1940), *Sandburg's Lincoln* (1974–1976), and *Gore Vidal's Lincoln* (1988). My goal in writing this book is to understand how different films, produced and consumed by different generations of Americans, have remembered and reinvented America's most beloved leader. The movies and miniseries examined in this book are arguably the most influential representations ever made about the most influential American who ever lived. They have much to teach us about Lincoln: not so much who he was, for that Lincoln is lost to history, but how we have chosen to remember and remake him. These films, therefore, also have much to teach us about ourselves.

Preface

The writing of this book would not have been possible without the help of several people, most notably Thomas W. Benson, who offered thoughtful suggestions and much-needed advice on earlier drafts.

Introduction

Lincoln in American Memory

> Lincoln the man was swallowed up by the myth, a myth that neither the passage of time nor the challenge of revision has been able to tarnish.
>
> —Harold Holzer, Gabor S. Boritt, and Mark E. Neely Jr., *Changing the Lincoln Image*

The story of Abraham Lincoln's life is familiar to most Americans. Not only major events of his political career but also minor details of his personal life are well known. The reasons for this cultural intimacy are many, but none matters more than this: Lincoln's life and death are more than history because they are more than *his* story. Rather, they are part of America's story—a tale that has been told and retold by successive generations eager to lay claim to a national ancestry that began with the Founding Fathers and is believed to have found greatness in a tall, thin midwesterner possessed of a shrill voice and a sound wisdom. Lincoln fought his way from poverty to glory, only to be stolen from us in the greatest of our national tragedies. Two centuries after his birth, Lincoln is remembered as our national icon because he gave a divided country unity, an enslaved people freedom, and a warring nation the hope of a lasting peace.

Lincoln made his debut on the national stage in the summer of 1858, when the lesser-known lawyer and legislator challenged the better-known Stephen A. Douglas for an Illinois Senate seat. Long Abe and the Little Giant clashed under the summer sun in no fewer than seven debates in just two months, capturing the interest of a nation that saw civil war on the horizon and felt a deep yearning for leadership. Since then, Lincoln's image has dominated the American imagination like no other figure, living or dead, resurfacing at least once a generation as if to remind the nation why it was worth saving.

Since Lincoln's assassination, countless speeches, poems, statues, songs, books, portraits, plays, and movies have been created. These tributes have both honored and altered his place in our memory. To this day, Lincoln's image flourishes in American memory, inspiring generations that measure and define themselves by the values and accomplishments they ascribe to their fallen idol.

The America that Lincoln loved and led has changed immeasurably since his lifetime, and so too has our image of Lincoln. The generations of Americans who have remade his image have conjured from one Lincoln many. The multiple incarnations of the man that are now so familiar in American culture and society began to emerge during his presidency, but they took permanent hold on the nation one evening in April 1865.

Assassination

At the moment of Lincoln's death, it is said, "Secretary of War Edwin M. Stanton, from his vigil at the foot of the bed, raised a hand and, tears streaming down his cheeks, declared, 'Now he belongs to the ages.'"[1] Stanton could not have comprehended the magnitude of his prophecy. Never before or since in American history has a man been memorialized more frequently or more gloriously than Abraham Lincoln. Nearly a century and a half since the evening of that fateful performance of *Our American Cousin,* Lincoln's image has refused to fade from the nation's mind. If anything, it has intensified.

The grounds for this intensification are not difficult to calculate. "One can begin with the appealing character of the man himself," historian Don E. Fehrenbacher observes, "the strangely moving quality of his prose, the dramatic perfection of a career rising from deep obscurity to exalted tragedy, the unique claims of the Civil War on American historical consciousness and of the Negro on America's collective consciousness."[2] In April 1865, just days after the president's death, Ralph Waldo Emerson foretold that Lincoln would "become mythological in a very few years."[3] The prediction was, in many respects, far from a long shot, but the speed and intensity with which it came to fruition likely would have astounded even Emerson. "The redefinition of Lincoln's place in American thought, his swift transcendence from history into folklore, was one of the more remarkable cultural phenomena of our history. It was the product of many influences, including religious fervor, superstition, the retrospective impact of Lincoln's own public utterances, and popular art."[4]

This transition from man to myth began the moment Booth's bullet found its mark. "The continent shook," one historian wrote, "as the news of Lincoln's assassination sped over it."[5] That Lincoln was shot on Good Friday was by no means lost on the citizens of his day. It underscored the inevitable comparisons to Christ, inspiring but one of many conceptions of Lincoln that to this day define not so much the man he was, but rather the manner in which successive generations have tended to remember him.

If the cannon blasts at Fort Sumter set in motion the battle that would dominate Lincoln's life, the firing of Booth's pistol started the war that would dominate him in death: the war to derive meaning from and attach meaning to Lincoln. Eulogizing the fallen president, the Reverend George H. Hepworth challenged: "Who shall dare deny that Lincoln dead may yet do more for America than Lincoln living?"[6] Thus began a national movement to conjure the spirit of Lincoln. Exactly how it would haunt generations of Americans could not have been known then, and it is only really beginning to reveal itself now. But this we do know: what Lincoln's ghost would come to mean for America would rival the impact of all of his earthly actions.

Centennial

On February 12, 1909, the United States celebrated a century of Lincoln. It is difficult to describe the jubilation felt by the country on the observation of his one hundredth birthday. Lincoln's centennial stands out as perhaps the most active moment in America's struggle to define his essence and his significance to the country. The centennial was the high-water mark of America's fascination with its sixteenth president, which reached a peak in the early decades of the twentieth century. No fewer than thirty-five statues of Lincoln were erected between 1900 and 1919, and his name was invoked an unprecedented 207 times in *The Congressional Record,* and

543 times in the *New York Times.*[7] Despite this, few twenty-first-century Americans know much about the centennial. The historical community laments that it was "one of those events that took up more space in the actual observance than it would in the historical record."[8]

In Hodgenville, Kentucky, Lincoln's birthplace was declared a national historic site. Theodore Roosevelt traveled to the remote site, where once stood Lincoln's one-room log cabin, to deliver an address in Lincoln's honor. Dozens of other national figures delivered similar speeches that day, including William Jennings Bryan in Springfield, Illinois, Joseph H. Choate at the Cooper Institute in New York City, and Booker T. Washington at the annual meeting of the Republican Club of New York City. Henry Cabot Lodge had expressed his desire that the festivities would begin a process that would finally "detach Lincoln from the myth, which has possession of all of us."[9] Cabot's wish would remain unfulfilled, however, as the occasion was observed in every part of the nation, including the deepest corners of the South, with parades, demonstrations, memorial services, and celebrations of Lincoln's life and legend that served only to exalt him to an ever more mythical proportion.

In spite of the spirit of inclusion that seems to have guided so many aspects of the celebration, all were not equal on that day. "For Negroes and their friends," historian Merrill D. Peterson writes, "Lincoln remained, above all, the Great Emancipator. They hoped to broadcast the message of racial justice and equality. But the commemoration, like everything else in American life, was Jim Crow, and to the Negro leaders who had long worshiped at Lincoln's shrine it seemed that 'the whites had outheralded Herod' on his anniversary."[10] But if the centennial anniversary had failed to initiate an era of justice and equality for all Americans, a memorial to Lincoln eventually would become ground zero for a national movement dedicated to both ideals.

Memorial

An interstate highway connecting Washington, D.C., to Gettysburg was the first proposal to receive serious consideration when the U.S. Congress decided to memorialize Abraham Lincoln. The proposal passed in the

Senate, but it was stopped by the House of Representatives, whose members apparently felt that marble was a more fitting medium than asphalt.[11] Once the commission assigned to plan a memorial had decided on a more traditional approach to commemoration, a swampy space at the end of the National Mall that faced the Washington Monument, and beyond that the Capitol Building, was selected. What to build there, however, was a matter not yet decided.

In the rhetoric of commemoration, nothingness counts for a great deal; silence and empty spaces, too, can be meaningful. Some thought that the chosen site was too far from the real action in Washington, too remote to attract the attention Lincoln deserved. But the commission wisely stuck to its plan. John Hay, Lincoln's personal secretary, explained: "Lincoln was of the immortals. You must not approach too close to the immortals. His monument should stand alone, remote from the common habitations of man, apart from the business and turmoil of the city; isolated, distinguished, and serene."[12]

The decision to locate the memorial in what was then relative isolation was the first step toward answering one of the most difficult questions at hand: which Lincoln to honor, the commoner or the statesman? Lincoln's image had long been pulled in opposing directions. It was a dilemma as old as the form of government that Lincoln had come to represent: "the tension between democracy's conflicting need for leaders with whom the masses can identify and leaders whom they can revere."[13] Eventually the tension became so great that it caused his image to fracture into the countless manifestations we know today: Honest Abe, the Great Emancipator, the Great Commoner, the Savior of the Union, the Self-Made Man, the First American, Lincoln the humorist and storyteller, Lincoln the fighter, and so on.

This was the challenge faced by every artist who would attempt to represent Lincoln in every medium. Thus, artistic representations of Lincoln usually focused on one aspect, sacrificing either his commonness or his greatness, which often left a figure that looked half drawn. Those who attempted to reconcile the inherent contradiction in Lincoln's dualism usually found themselves with something resembling "a Gilbert Stuart painting with a halo dubbed in by later, less skillful hands."[14] The best-known riddle in Washington, D.C., has long been: Who is buried in Grant's tomb? But in 1922, the more enigmatic question might have been: Who will be enshrined in Lincoln's memorial?

It was of course the godly statesman, and not the homely frontiersman, preserved for future generations in the intimidating monument eventually approved by the Lincoln Memorial Commission. The celebration of Lincoln's humble origins would have to be taken up by lesser sites, such as his birthplace in Kentucky. In Washington, the gigantic Greek-inspired neoclassical structure reflected not only the epic enlargement that Lincoln's reputation had enjoyed to that point, but also a young country's gathering sense of history and purpose. In fairness, the design did make some effort to reflect the paradoxical nature of Lincoln's image. The hands of his statue, for example, offer insight to the tourist willing and able to read them. With one hand relaxed and the other clenched in a fist, the figure may be read as a reflection of Lincoln's desire for peace as well as his willingness to fight for it. Nevertheless, the memorial marked a clear choice in the interpretation of Lincoln that has had a lasting effect. The Great Commoner will be forever remembered, first and foremost, as one of history's great men, with his commonness demoted to a charming ancillary attribute.

On May 30, 1922, former U.S. president and chairman of the Lincoln Memorial Commission, William Howard Taft, presided over the monument's dedication. In a speech ripe with religious symbolism, Taft proclaimed: "Here is a shrine at which all can worship. Here is an altar upon which the sacrifice was made in the cause of Liberty. Here a sacred religious refuge in which those who love country and love God can find inspiration and repose."[15]

Although the civil rights movement of the 1960s would forever alter the meaning of the Lincoln Memorial, the statue was in fact erected to subvert controversy and avoid debate. In that regard, it failed miserably. If the battle over the memorial's design had been hard fought, the battle to interpret it began even before the last stone was laid. "Conceived and dedicated as holy ground, the Lincoln Memorial became, as early as 1922, racially contested ground. By chance or design, the shrine straddled boundaries: between North and South, between black and white, and between official and vernacular memory. As both temple and tourist attraction, it sat on the cusp between sacred and secular."[16] Today the memorial remains a symbolic sight for all who look back to Lincoln as they struggle to move the country forward.

Civil Rights

On February 12, 1959, Lincoln turned 150. President Eisenhower created the Lincoln Sesquicentennial Commission, which adopted the theme "Lincoln: Symbol of the Free Man" and prepared a schedule of events that would highlight Lincoln's dedication to democracy.[17] The event did not rival the spectacle of the centennial celebration fifty years earlier, nor could it compete with the symbolic import of the dedication of the Lincoln Memorial of thirty-seven years before. In part, this was due to other commitments to national commemoration. The 1930s had witnessed the bicentennial anniversaries of the births of both George Washington and Thomas Jefferson. In addition, the country was already anticipating the 1961 centennial anniversary of the outbreak of the Civil War, which would of course bring with it another round of all things Lincoln. The 150th anniversary of his birth was observed, but it did not leave a permanent mark upon the nation, nor did it alter Lincoln's memory in any significant way.

If in the 1950s Lincoln had become a supporting character in the American narrative, the 1960s would hand him yet another starring role. When Martin Luther King Jr. shared his dream of racial equality, he did so with the Great Emancipator watching approvingly over his shoulder. Lincoln's silent participation in the civil rights movement was inevitable—not merely because of his role in the abolition of slavery but also because the decade in which America lost two Kennedys and a King also observed the centennial mark of Lincoln's own tragic assassination. The anniversary of Lincoln's death obviously did not offer the country an occasion for celebration, as had previous Lincoln anniversaries. It was instead a moment that called a country about to be accused of giving its people of color a check marked "insufficient funds" to reflect upon all that Lincoln had given the nation, and all that its citizens still owed to one another.

The turbulent 1960s also marked one hundred years since the signing of the Emancipation Proclamation, the utterance of the Gettysburg Address, the end of the Civil War, and the passage of the Thirteenth Amendment—reasons all for the nation to remember with fondness and gratitude the one man most responsible for each of these achievements.

However, not all were enamored of the Great Emancipator, including even some who favored the cause championed by King. After all, it was during his debates with Stephen Douglas that Lincoln had proclaimed: "I agree that the negro may not be my equal . . . in many respects—certainly not in color, and in intellectual development, perhaps."[18] What historian Don E. Fehrenbacher and others call the "anti-Lincoln tradition" has been with us since the Northern states ensured his election to the presidency with little assistance from the South.[19] Still, whatever Americans thought of Lincoln's true feelings on race, it was clear to all in the 1960s that preaching the gospel of Lincoln was among the most powerful means available for converting nonbelievers to the cause of racial equality.

The civil rights movement, in employing Lincoln to change its own public image, also changed Lincoln's image. Between the years 1939 and 1963, when the famous March for Jobs and Freedom occurred, activists regularly identified their cause as an extension of Lincoln's own work, often locating their efforts at the Lincoln Memorial. What came of the fight for civil rights is known to most Americans, but its consequences for Lincoln were less clear then, and remain so now.

"The U.S. Congress," Barry Schwartz notes, "with the full support of its Southern members, had built the Lincoln Memorial to celebrate regional, not racial, unity."[20] On this the memorial itself could not have been clearer. The inscription above Daniel Chester French's towering statue reads: "In This Temple as in the Hearts of the People for Whom He Saved the Union the Memory of Abraham Lincoln Is Enshrined Forever." This rhetoric was anything but accidental. "Art critic Royal Cortissoz wrote these lines and explained their subtlety to [the memorial's architect Henry] Bacon: 'The memorial must make a common ground for the meeting of the north and the south. By emphasizing his saving the union you appeal to both sections. By saying nothing of slavery you avoid the rubbing of old sores.'"[21] Thus, it was the Lincoln who preserved the Union, not the Lincoln who freed the slaves, whom the Congress had intended to honor.

The civil rights movement changed this, effectively reversing the way Americans interpret that sacred spot on the west end of the National Mall. What had been a temple of the Savior of the Union was transformed into a shrine of the Great Emancipator. It was done with such success that a plaque has been placed on the steps of the memorial to mark the spot on which King delivered his famous "I Have a Dream" speech, second only in the annals of American oratory to Lincoln's own words at Gettysburg. The monument to the Civil War president now also memorialized the civil rights leader. Two men and one cause are now forever joined; as the civil rights movement co-opted the memorial to represent its own mission, the hierarchy of Lincoln's most significant achievements has been permanently rearranged.

If any were tempted to cry foul over the alterations to Lincoln's place in history, they must not have realized that civil rights leaders had simply taken a page from Lincoln's own playbook. Garry Wills argues that in just 272 words—the sum of the Gettysburg Address—Lincoln "remade America."[22] He did so, in part, by changing the way nineteenth-century Americans remembered their eighteenth-century revolutionary forebears. "Four score and seven years ago, our fathers brought forth on this continent, a new nation, conceived in liberty, and dedicated to the proposition that all men are created equal." With these words Lincoln began to revise the memory of the Founding Fathers, who were in Lincoln's time as he is in ours: national icons, beloved and revered, but not necessarily understood. Although the Constitution they created does indeed state that "all men are created equal," the framers gave no indication that this birthright extended to persons of color. Yet Lincoln understood that this detail was not conducive to his efforts to characterize the cause of the North as an extension of their work. History, therefore, would have to change, and there seemed no better place to revise it than at Gettysburg. The musket and the cannonball could not accomplish what Lincoln's fiery rhetoric would do in only a matter of minutes.

> He would cleanse the Constitution—not, as William Lloyd Garrison had, by burning an instrument that countenanced slavery. He altered the document from within, by appeal from its letter to the

> spirit, subtly changing the recalcitrant stuff of that legal compromise, bringing it to its own indictment. By implicitly doing this, he performed one of the most daring acts of open-air sleight-of-hand ever witnessed by the unsuspecting. Everyone in that vast throng of thousands was having his or her intellectual pocket picked. The crowd departed with a new thing in its ideological luggage, that new constitution Lincoln had substituted for the one they brought there with them. They walked off, from those curving graves on the hillside, under a changed sky, into a different America. Lincoln had revolutionized the Revolution, giving people a new past to live with that would change their future indefinitely.[23]

Lincoln himself, therefore, was a revisionist historian.

For more than a century and a half Americans have held Lincoln as a national ideal, looking to him each time they wish to take stock of who they are and whom they should hope to become. Yet, as noted above, this habit has caused Lincoln's image to become increasingly fractured and complex. Each time Lincoln's memory is evoked, it is also changed. If indeed Americans do define themselves through their depictions of their national icon, they too are changed by each new Lincoln they create.

Public Memory

The sociologist Maurice Halbwachs is often identified as the father of public or collective memory studies. His landmark work, *On Collective Memory,* drew important distinctions between individual and collective memory, emphasizing that remembering is not only an individual act, that different groups of people can have different collective memories about the same shared past, and that these collective memories are always subject to revision. In the individual mind, Halbwachs argued, "the past is not preserved but is reconstructed on the basis of the present." At the societal level, the process is even more complex, involving "the instruments used by the collective memory to reconstruct an image of the past which is in accord, in each epoch, with the predominant thoughts of the society."[24]

The historian John Bodnar offers a more recent definition of the focus and functions of public memory in his landmark book, *Remaking America:* "Public memory is a body of beliefs and ideas about the past that help a public or society understand both its past, present, and by implication, its future. It is fashioned ideally in a public sphere in which various parts of the social structure exchange views. The major focus of this communicative and cognitive process is not the past, however, but serious matters in the present such as the nature of power and the question of loyalty to both official and vernacular cultures."[25]

In spite of the elegant simplicity of Bodnar's definition, Michael Kammen articulates the complex challenge of understanding the role of public memory within a specific cultural context (the United States, in his study) in his own landmark text, *Mystic Chords of Memory:*

> Public memory, which contains a slowly shifting configuration of traditions, is ideologically important because it shapes a nation's ethos and sense of identity. That explains, at least in part, why memory is always selective and is so often contested. Although there have been a great many political conflicts concerning American traditions, ultimately there is a powerful tendency in the United States to depoliticize traditions for the sake of "reconciliation." Consequently the politics of culture in this country has everything to do with the process of contestation *and* with the subsequent quest for reconciliation. Memory is more likely to be activated by contestation, and amnesia is more likely to be induced by the desire for reconciliation.[26]

Building on Halbwachs's pioneering work, academics like Bodnar and Kammen began to question long-standing assumptions about the past and its relation to the present.

In recent years, the field has flourished. "Interdisciplinary work in memory studies," Gary R. Edgerton reports, "now boasts adherents in American studies, anthropology, communication, cultural studies, English, history, psychology and sociology."[27] The result is a diverse and ever-growing body of interdisciplinary research on public memory.[28] Kendall R. Phillips suggests that we may divide much of the transdisciplinary scholarship in public memory into the broad categories of "the memory of publics" and "the publicness of memory."[29] Carole Blair, Greg Dickinson, and Brian L. Ott note that although public memory scholarship includes diverse work from divergent disciplines, memory studies as a whole is not without its common assumptions. These include: "(1) memory is activated by present concerns, issues, or anxieties; (2) memory narrates shared identities, constructing senses of communal belonging; (3) memory is animated by affect; (4) memory is partial, partisan, and thus often contested; (5) memory relies on material and/or symbolic supports; (6) memory has a history."[30]

Communication technologies, from the printing press to smart phones, have been particularly influential forces in shaping public memory. "Technologies of mass culture have been called on to play a new and important role in circulating images and narratives about the past," Alison Landsberg argues, and "rather than disdain the new memory-making technologies, we must instead recognize their power and political potential."[31] Barbie Zelizer argues that image-based technologies are especially powerful in the formation and contestation of public memories, as they "constitute a cogent means of tackling the past and making it work for the present."[32]

Within the broad category of visual media, film and television are recognized as perhaps the most persuasive, regarded by many as "the archetype[s] of the new technologies of memory created in the twentieth century."[33] Historians like John E. O'Connor, Peter C. Rollins, and Robert Brent Toplin have contributed tremendously and more recently to the conversation, producing a wealth of important scholarship in the area of film and history.[34] As historians, their work leans toward measuring historical films against the written historical record as created by historians, a task that is at least slightly different than interrogating films in the context of public memory.

In his book *Memory and Popular Film,* Paul Grainge makes the case for examining films about the past through the lens of memory studies, which "draws attention to the activations and eruptions of the past as they are experienced in and constituted by the present."[35] Grainge's approach is not new but rather a recent and interesting example of what some in the humanities have been doing for decades. Indeed, many of the most revered thinkers of the twentieth century have theorized the ways in which moving images resonate with our sense of public history and the role of public memory, including Guy Debord (who was also a filmmaker), Gilles Deleuze, Michel Foucault, and Frederic Jameson. Their scholarship on film, history, and memory is far too complex even to summarize here, but suffice to say that collectively their work demonstrates that visual, narrative media possess an awesome power to show people "not what they were, but what they must remember having been."[36]

Given the unending attention that academics award to Abraham Lincoln, and given the recent multidisciplinary attention granted to films about the past, it would seem obvious that films about Lincoln would be a popular topic in the literature on film, history, and memory. And yet they are not. We have not ignored Lincoln's evolving image in American public memory altogether. In fact, the genre of Lincoln literature now includes no shortage of books whose subject is not the man but rather the myth.[37] It is a fascinating area of Lincoln studies, but one that routinely ignores anything that might be characterized as popular culture.

Merrill Peterson's *Lincoln in American Memory,* for example, which might be the most thorough and authoritative tome ever written on the subject of Lincoln's evolving image, is just shy of four hundred pages. Of these, he devotes fewer than three pages to discussing the influence of films such as *Young Mr. Lincoln,* which have been consumed by millions of viewers across several generations. The few book-length studies of Lincoln representations in popular culture tend to lack any theoretical foundation or critical method.[38] The few article-length or chapter-length studies published throughout the twentieth century have made more thoughtful contributions to our understanding of Lincoln's image, but of course the constraints of space have limited what these texts are able to offer.[39] Indeed, Hollywood's Lincoln is an area of Lincoln studies and memory studies that demands attention.

Bicentennial

On January 24, 2000, HR 1451 was introduced in the U.S. Congress. The bill proposed the creation of an official commission to prepare for Lincoln's two hundredth birthday. The Abraham Lincoln Bicentennial Commission Act was approved on February 25, 2000, thereby creating the Abraham Lincoln Bicentennial Commission. The legislation called not only for the general promotion all of things Lincoln but also for such specific acts as the issuance of bicentennial postage stamps, the minting of five bicentennial pennies, and the rededication of the Lincoln Memorial in Washington, D.C. The Bicentennial Commission hoped that in addition to its own national efforts, state and local governments would participate as well, so that the countless Lincoln statues keeping watch over courthouse lawns and public squares throughout the country could shine more brightly as they were readied to be rediscovered and rededicated.

Amazingly, when February 12, 2009, finally arrived, almost no one noticed. If the 1959 sesquicentennial had paled in comparison to the 1909 centennial, the 2009 bicentennial was nearly invisible. Distracted by a contentious national election, two unpopular wars, and a historic collapse of the national economy, the Union that Lincoln had once saved was perhaps too busy trying to save itself yet again. It was nothing less than remarkable that the 2008 election of Barack Obama, an Illinois native and the country's first African American president, did not serve as a catalyst for the greatest of all Lincoln celebrations. But when the bicentennial anniversary of Lincoln's birth came and went with so little attention, even the faithful must have questioned whether Lincoln's rich cultural currency had finally run out.

If the public at large did not respond to the call of the Bicentennial Commission, the intellectual community did. The already swollen river of Lincoln literature was flooded yet again with a tidal wave of new manuscripts. Doris Kearns Goodwin's *Team of Rivals,* published in the fall of 2005, signaled to the literary community that the genre of Lincoln had returned. Countless titles followed, in which Lincoln was praised, blamed, and even outed as a closeted homosexual.[40] The streets may not have been lined with citizens eager to celebrate Lincoln, but at least the bookshelves were lined with new volumes determined to further our understanding of him.

Suspiciously absent from all of this, though, was any contribution from the nation's unofficial historian and storyteller: Hollywood. But 2012 would change that, and it would change Lincoln too.

1

Great Emancipator

Lincoln before *Lincoln* (2012)

> Hollywood has had a profound impact on the way we think about the presidents who lived before Hollywood came into existence. In the absence of actual footage of these presidents, we have allowed Hollywood to fill in the blanks in our minds.
>
> —Richard Shenkman, *Hollywood's White House*

Movie audiences must have thought that they were seeing double in 2012. After decades without a major Lincoln movie and years of rumors about a Spielberg-directed biography, audiences were treated to no fewer than two feature films about America's most popular president. On their surface, the acclaimed *Lincoln* (2012) and the absurd *Abraham Lincoln: Vampire Hunter* (2012) could not have been more different. Indeed, the former was based on an award-winning biography penned by a Harvard historian, while the latter was scripted by the writer responsible for *Pride and Prejudice and Zombies.*[1] But despite their obvious differences, the two films presented essentially the same character: a heroic Lincoln who fought for the weak and freed the enslaved. And it was a radical moment for Honest Abe in Hollywood. For all the Lincolns who had appeared on-screen, never before had the Great Emancipator been given a starring role.

Hollywood's Historical Heroes

The cinema emerged in the 1890s and quickly became a popular and affordable form of mass entertainment. That it would turn rather quickly to the remarkable life of Abraham Lincoln should not have come as a surprise. After all, it was not uncommon then, nor is it now, for Hollywood to look to the library for inspiration. Tales of heroes and villains, both factual and fictional, offered familiar content and completed story lines. They were tantalizing to the early studios, eager to capitalize on the public's growing hunger for motion pictures. Moreover, the first film audiences saw the medium not as an art form but as a novelty—the spectacle of moving pictures. The entertainment value of the flickies came not from the joy of a new form of narrative, nor from the use of sophisticated cinematic techniques. The thrill came instead from seeing stationary images suddenly come to life—and who better to resurrect than Lincoln?

Perhaps the most celebrated subgenre of historical movies is the life of the great man or woman. Biographical pictures, or biopics, are not only popular, they are also consequential. They tend to endorse a particular kind of life as more interesting, more admirable, more memorable than others. "Thoughts about society are almost always invested in personal images," sociologist and Lincoln scholar Barry Schwartz argues. "History is realized in the same way: remembrance of the past begins with the remembrance of men."[2] By choosing to remember certain types of men and women, the entertainment industry would do much more than just entertain the public. It would, by accident or design, teach generations of film and television viewers exactly which sorts of lives are worth living—and reliving.

In his definitive study of the genre, George F. Custen notes that most of Hollywood's biographical films consist of four basic narrative elements.[3] The first is that biopics almost always begin in medias res—in the middle of things. Although this is primarily the result of having to review an entire life in just an hour or two, it is also consequential, suggesting a sense of inevitability. Hollywood's historical figures seem destined for greatness from the very moment that we meet them. Their lives and their place in history are preordained.

The second element is the absence of immediate family members. Alone in the world, the protagonist is presented as a self-made man or woman. Greatness is thus portrayed as the result of both destiny and self-determination. According to Hollywood, heroes are born, not made. The third element in the classic Hollywood biopic is a heterosexual romance that humanizes the character and often forces a pivotal choice between love and career. An inclination toward personal sacrifice is therefore essential for Hollywood's historical heroes, who are tempted with the personal pleasures of family or fortune but choose the good of others, if not of all humankind.

Finally, biopics almost always climax with an act of dual judgment. This pivotal moment often assumes the form of a public event, such as a speech or trial, in which the person is judged both morally and professionally by other characters in the film and by the audience. For the latter, these moments offer not only an invitation to evaluate the life of the person portrayed on-screen but also as an opportunity to evaluate their own lives. It is here that the lessons learned from the lives of great men and women are held up as a model for viewers to follow.

The Reel Lincoln, Part I

Although the movies and miniseries examined closely in subsequent chapters are among the best known of all Lincoln films, they share the genre with many other titles, some of them obscure and a few that are undeniably strange. What follows here is a very brief, highly selective, and admittedly incomplete history of nondocumentary Lincoln films produced from the early to late twentieth century.[4]

Lincoln's debut in Hollywood was very likely in the Edison Film Company's production of *Uncle Tom's Cabin* (1903). Faithful to the famous Harriet Beecher Stowe novel from which it was adapted, the short film features Lincoln as only a minor character. But even if his portrayal was not significant, its timing was: less than a decade old, the cinema had discovered Lincoln. It is impossible to know how many early Hollywood films have been lost to history, including films about history. Therefore, we cannot know how many times Lincoln has appeared on the screen. However, at least some lost Lincoln films are known to have existed.

The Life of Abraham Lincoln (1908), *The Blue and the Grey; or, The Days of '61* (1908), *The Sleeping Sentinel* (1910), *Grant and Lincoln* (1911), *When Lincoln Was President* (1913), and *The Battle of Gettysburg* (1913) are just a few of the early Lincoln films for which we have a paper trail but no celluloid. One can only speculate about how exactly Lincoln was represented in these films, as well as how many other lost Lincoln films were once eagerly watched by early audiences. Although *The Birth of a Nation* (1915)—examined in detail in chapter 2—is the most influential silent film to feature Lincoln, there were several others of that era that explored Lincoln's life in much greater detail.

The Seventh Son (1912), also a lost Lincoln film, is the first known to combine the familiar pardon story with a variation on what is now the well-known story of Mrs. Bixby. In 1864, the historical Lincoln was made aware of a woman from Boston, Mrs. Bixby, who had lost five sons fighting for the Union army. Although historians disagree on the matter of authorship, Mrs. Bixby was sent a letter, possibly written by Lincoln himself. The short note offered consolation to the grieving mother and "the thanks of a grateful nation for having laid so costly a sacrifice upon the altar of freedom." The letter was soon reprinted in newspapers and remains a famous, if historically suspect, Lincoln artifact. *The Seventh Son* offers a variation of this tale, as did the successful Steven Spielberg film, *Saving Private Ryan* (1998), in which a military officer actually reads aloud to soldiers the letter to Mrs. Bixby.

Among the more unusual early Lincoln films was *Lincoln the Lover* (1914). Ralph Ince, who played Lincoln in *The Seventh Son,* both directed and starred in this short. According to Mark S. Reinhart, it was the first film ever to explore Lincoln's private life.[5] Interestingly, the film says nothing of Lincoln's turbulent relationship with wife Mary Todd, instead concentrating solely on a historically suspect relationship he might have had in New Salem with a woman named Ann Rutledge. The courtship comes to the viewer by means of a flashback, as President Lincoln is shown recalling earlier days. Faithful to the legend, the film shows Lincoln and Rutledge falling in love and planning to marry. However, Ann dies suddenly, leaving the young Lincoln devastated.

Historians agree that a woman named Ann Rutledge lived in New Salem at the time Lincoln lived there, and thus it is possible that the two would have known one another. However, it is in no way certain that a romantic relationship ever materialized. Despite this, *Lincoln the Lover* is an important part of a tradition among Hollywood biopics of featuring the romance as a historical fact. The romance almost always serves to highlight one of the narrative elements Custen identified, showcasing Lincoln's renunciation of his personal desires to pursue a career as public servant.

Lincoln for the Defense (1913) and *The Land of Opportunity* (1920) are important films because, like John Ford's *Young Mr. Lincoln* (1939), they concern themselves not with Lincoln's political accomplishments but rather with his legal career. In fact, all three films present modified versions of the famous Armstrong case.[6] In 1857, while practicing law in Springfield, Illinois, Lincoln agreed to defend a young man, Duff Armstrong, who had been accused of murder. Lincoln successfully and famously secured Armstrong's acquittal by offering "proof" that a key witness was lying when he claimed to have observed the killing. The witness insisted that he could see the murder because the full moon offered sufficient light. Lincoln used the *Farmer's Almanac* to show that the moon was not full and indeed very low in the sky on the date and time in question. The details of the trial are the subject of continual debate among historians, but Hollywood seems to have made up its mind that the Armstrong case was Lincoln's shining moment in the courtroom, and a promise of even greater things to come.

Although each of the aforementioned films is significant within the whole of the Lincoln genre, none can compare to *The Cycle of Photodramas Based on the Adventures of Abraham Lincoln. The Lincoln Cycle,* as it is known, is easily the most ambitious effort ever to chronicle Lincoln's life on film. Created by Lincoln impersonator Benjamin Chapin, *The Lincoln Cycle* was conceived as a series of films that would portray Lincoln's life from birth to death. Starting in 1913, Chapin shot footage for multiple films, even securing President Woodrow Wilson's permission to film some scenes at the White House.[7]

The first film to be released, *Old Abe* (1915), concentrated on the frontier life of Lincoln's grandfather. The largely fictional plot stressed a commonly evoked but historically unsubstantiated connection between Lincoln's grandfather and Daniel Boone. In 1917, he released four films simultaneously: *My Mother, My Father, Myself,* and *The Call to Arms.*

The films ran successfully in New York, which helped Chapin secure a deal to release *Son of Democracy* (1918) the following year.[8] This feature consisted of the four short films shown in New York along with most of Chapin's remaining Lincoln footage, taking Lincoln up to the early years of his presidency. But unlike Chapin's previous efforts, *Son of Democracy* was neither profitable nor well received by critics. Chapin was nonetheless determined to continue chronicling Lincoln's life, but he died of tuberculosis the following year. Despite Chapin's ambition and his early success, the collection of films known as *The Lincoln Cycle* has faded into history and today exerts little influence over how Lincoln is remembered.

Another once-important film whose significance has diminished over time is *The Dramatic Life of Abraham Lincoln* (1924). Along with D. W. Griffith's *Abraham Lincoln* (1930), it is one of only a few feature-length films to follow Lincoln from birth to death. Directed by Phil Rosen and featuring George Billings in the title role, the film is regarded as one of the best produced of its era. Producers Al and Ray Rockett promoted the film by boasting that their extensive research into Lincoln's life had helped them to create the most historically accurate film to date.[9] Despite this, several popular but inaccurate Lincoln myths were included, such as the notion that Lincoln delivered his famous Gettysburg Address impromptu. The film later enjoyed a brief second life when an edited version was released by Eastman Teaching Films. Retitled more simply *Abraham Lincoln* (1933), the thirty-minute short was designed to be a classroom teaching tool, further muddling the line between Lincoln films as mass entertainment and as education.

Although the quality of these early silent films cannot compare with those made in later years, the films of this early era are significant for at least two reasons. First, more films were made about Lincoln during this time than at any other in history, and that is not surprising. Although Lincoln is to us a remote figure from the distant past, the same cannot be said for film audiences in the early years of the twentieth century. Many audience members had been alive when Lincoln was in the White House, and for the rest, Lincoln's life and legacy were subjects likely discussed with great regularity. To us, Lincoln is a character. To them, he had been a man, a president, *their* president. Second, not only had Hollywood discovered Lincoln early in its existence, it was already freely mixing historical fact with creative fiction as it represented him on the screen. This would set a tone for how future generations of filmmakers and audiences would think about Lincoln. To this day, it is clear that filmmakers look to early silent films like Griffith's *The Birth of a Nation* for guidance and inspiration when attempting to tell Lincoln's tale yet again.

The Reel Lincoln, Part II

If the silent cinema was stylistically conservative in its treatment of Lincoln, the early sound and television eras were marked by narrative and stylistic experimentation. For example, a most uncommon Lincoln is found in the film *Of Human Hearts* (1938). Featuring John Carradine as Lincoln as well as Jimmy Stewart and Walter Huston (who had played Lincoln in Griffith's 1930 biopic), the narrative is quite simply bizarre. Stewart plays a medic in the Union army who rarely takes the time to respond to the many letters he receives from his mother. Thinking that her son must be dead, the mother writes to President Lincoln, who not only reads the letter but sends for Stewart. Lincoln proceeds to scold him "with a fury seldom seen in the history of Lincoln screen portrayals."[10]

The Tall Target (1951) is one of the more eerie films ever made about Lincoln. Focusing on the alleged Baltimore Plot, it tells the story of a young police detective trying to prevent an assassination attempt as Lincoln travels from Illinois to Washington for his 1861 inauguration. Part of what makes the film eerie, at least for the modern viewer, is not the macabre plot but rather the detective's name: John Kennedy. Released a decade before the real John Kennedy was elected president, the choice of name obviously was not an attempt to draw yet one more connection between the two assassinated presidents. Still, in the mind of the modern viewer, the film resonates strongly with popular Lincoln/Kennedy conspiracy theories.

The early 1950s saw the new medium of television take a strong interest in Lincoln, just as the cinema had done a half century earlier. Although it is tempting to assume that Lincoln's irresistible character and remarkable life were responsible for this revival, the focus on Lincoln in early television likely had more to do with the challenges of the new technology.

New forms of communication technology tend to rely, at least initially, on existing forms of technology when developing both their style and content. For instance, when the cinema emerged in the 1890s, it borrowed heavily from the look of theater and the pages of popular literature. Television would do the same, looking at lot like live theater and radio, and flooding the early airwaves with stories already popular in other media. In light of the success enjoyed in the 1930s and 1940s by filmmakers interested in Lincoln, it is no wonder that Long Abe quickly appeared on the small screen.

Popular television programs such as *You Are There, Wide, Wide World, American Inventory, Show of the Month, American Heritage, TV Reader's Digest,* and *Cavalcade of America* all devoted episodes to familiar events in Lincoln's life. Even fantastical television series, such as *The Twilight Zone* and *Star Trek,* found absurdly creative ways to work Lincoln into their narratives. Many of these early Lincoln television portrayals, while not necessarily remarkable in and of themselves, anticipated the television miniseries of the 1970s and 1980s, which shaped a whole new generation's sense of itself in relation to Lincoln.

Likely the most ambitious Lincoln-themed undertaking in early television was *Abraham Lincoln: The Early Years.* A series of five half-hour episodes that aired on CBS in 1952, *The Early Years* was, in a sense, the realization of what Benjamin Chapin had tried but failed to produce in *The Lincoln Cycle:* a multitext docudrama that dug deep into Lincoln. Although not as grand in scope as Chapin's project, *Abraham Lincoln: The Early Years* "remains one of the finest Lincoln-related works ever to be produced."[11]

In the turbulent 1960s, the nation mourned the loss of two Kennedys and King, and it struggled with a military war abroad and a culture war at home. American popular culture reflected in this era a renewed interest in Abraham Lincoln. In 1964, NBC aired a version of Robert Sherwood's *Abe Lincoln in Illinois.* Although unremarkable in its depiction of Lincoln, the program is vitally important in that it was written and directed by George Schaefer, who later directed *Sandburg's Lincoln* (1974–1976). The next year saw the release of *The Great Debate: Lincoln versus Douglas* (1965). This film is interesting for at least one reason: Lincoln was portrayed by Hal

Holbrook, who would later wear the stovepipe hat in both *Sandburg's Lincoln* and *North and South* (1985) and who would play a small role in Spielberg's *Lincoln* in 2012.

The following decade showed no decline in our national obsession with Lincoln, both on television and within the larger American culture. As 1976 drew closer and America prepared to celebrate its bicentennial, the country began once again to take stock of itself and its heroes. Lincoln, naturally, resurfaced as the enduring symbol of all that is great about the nation he preserved. In *Abraham Lincoln on the Screen,* Mark S. Reinhart catalogs no fewer than nineteen movies, miniseries, documentaries, television episodes, and educational shorts produced between 1970 and 1976. More amazing than the sheer number of such productions is their range, which spans the conventional to the controversial and covers nearly everything in between.

The Selling of Abe Lincoln, 1976 (1974) paints a portrait of Lincoln like nothing else ever seen on film or television. The hour-long drama, produced by and shown on a Chicago public TV station, amounts to an extended meditation on the possibilities and limitations of political advertising on television. The broadcast imagines Lincoln as a modern-day political candidate struggling with the pressure to compromise his moral commitments in the rough-and-tumble of a modern mass-mediated campaign. In the end, Lincoln cannot decide if TV ads are an acceptable way in which to express his deeply held social and political views.

The Lincoln Conspiracy (1977) was based upon a nonfiction book of the same name. Both book and film claim, among other things, that Lincoln's own secretary of war, Edwin M. Stanton, conspired to have Lincoln kidnapped, and that John Wilkes Booth was in fact not killed at the Garrett farm in Virginia. The plot of film and book alike is absurd, and both have come to be regarded as promoting one of the "worst historical abuses ever perpetrated in a Lincoln-related motion picture."[12]

These controversial depictions are balanced by several others that are far more traditional. One notable example is the made-for-television movie *The Day Lincoln Was Shot* (1998), based on a 1955 novel by Jim Bishop. Featuring veteran character actor Lance Henriksen in the title role, the movie depicted the events that led up to and came after Lincoln's assassination. The story had appeared on television before, when Raymond Massey performed the title role in a 1956 live television broadcast. In both versions, Booth is presented as a classic cinematic villain and Lincoln as a nearly divine tragic hero.

Despite such variance in content and quality of Lincoln portrayals, the second half of the twentieth century witnessed at least two notable trends. First, it is clear that neither America's fascination with Abraham Lincoln nor its appetite for Lincoln movies diminished as his death moved beyond the centennial mark. If anything, they grew more intense. Second, it is equally clear that the most creative and memorable Lincoln representations from the 1950s forward were found not in the movie theater but on the television screen. This trend would continue, climaxing during the 1970s and 1980s golden era of the TV miniseries and relenting only in the second decade of the new century, when Lincoln finally returned to the big screen.

2012

In 2009, an unknown writer named Seth Grahame-Smith published what would become a best-selling cult novel, *Pride and Prejudice and Zombies.* The generic mash-up gave Grahame-Smith, who had earned a degree in film from Emerson College, his first real literary success. The book, which lists Jane Austen as coauthor, was quickly optioned by a major film studio, although today the project remains mired in preproduction.

Grahame-Smith next penned another future cult classic, one that Hollywood would waste no time in bringing to the big screen: *Abraham Lincoln: Vampire Hunter.* The adaptation was produced by Tim Burton and took the form of an action-horror hybrid that cast Lincoln as a secret assassin who battles vampires, destroying the creatures who feed on the blood of slaves, and with them the need for slavery itself. Although the film performed well in theaters, it was universally panned by critics, who objected not to its historical absurdity but rather to what they saw as a dearth of artistic merit. Whatever the critics thought, audiences loved it. After a half century without a major theatrically released film, Lincoln was back. And he was pissed.

Just four months after *Abraham Lincoln: Vampire Hunter* appeared in theaters, audiences were offered a far more reverent Lincoln film. Rumors of a Spielberg-directed Lincoln picture had circulated in Hollywood for nearly a decade, ever since Spielberg had optioned the rights to Doris Kearns Goodwin's 2005 biography, *Team of Rivals: The Political Genius of Abraham Lincoln*.[13] The film was scripted by Tony Kushner and starred Daniel Day Lewis as Lincoln. The narrative focused on the final months of Lincoln's life, including and especially the passage of the Thirteenth Amendment, the end of the Civil War, and the buildup to Lincoln's assassination. To say that it was an enormous success, both financially and critically, would be an understatement. The film was nominated for dozens of awards, and it grossed nearly $300 million.

For the purposes of this project, what matters more than the many stark and obvious differences between Spielberg's *Lincoln* and *Abraham Lincoln: Vampire Hunter* is the one thing they share in common: a focus on Lincoln as the Great Emancipator. Beginning with D. W. Griffith's *The Birth of a Nation*—an overtly racist film that laments the demise of the Confederacy and celebrates the formation of the Ku Klux Klan—Hollywood routinely minimized or simply ignored Lincoln's role as the emancipator. As the following chapters in this book make clear, Lincoln has enjoyed many incarnations: Savior of the Union, Great Commoner, and the First American, among others. Before 2012, Hollywood had celebrated them all but neglected one: Lincoln as the Great Emancipator.

Like the famous Lincoln Memorial in Washington, D.C., Hollywood subtly reinforced the notion that freeing the slaves was not among Lincoln's most significant achievements. By accident or design, American movies and miniseries routinely left the emancipator on the cutting room floor while giving a starring role to one of Lincoln's other manifestations. It was a century-long act of historical revision and powerful memory work likely to have shaped how several generations of Americans understood both Lincoln and his relation to race. And although it came to a very visible end in 2012, it leaves us to ask: How did popular movies and miniseries invite Americans to understand themselves and to remember Lincoln before *Lincoln*?

2

Great Heart

The Birth of a Nation (1915)

> The reputation of the martyred . . . president . . . is in many ways a construction, created by different people in different ways at different times. The portrayal of Lincoln in *The Birth of a Nation* both reflected and influenced that process of construction.
>
> —Melvyn Stokes, *DW Griffith's "The Birth of a Nation"*

This chapter examines D. W. Griffith's infamous film, *The Birth of a Nation*, concentrating on perhaps the only element not yet fully understood: the film's consequential construction of Abraham Lincoln. In the two hundred years since his birth, Lincoln has been everywhere in American culture, including mainstream film and television. The movies and miniseries about Lincoln's life and death have been watched by many but studied by few. They continue to be consumed for pleasure yet dismissed as mere entertainment. They have introduced and reintroduced the most famous of all Americans to millions of viewers who believe beyond doubt that all that is good in America came from, or was made better by, their beloved Lincoln. Interestingly, many of these same viewers also believe that the popular media they so enthusiastically consume could not possibly influence their attitudes toward any serious subject, least of all their sense of Lincoln. Our tendency to deny the power of popular culture only adds to its potency. *The Birth of a Nation* set the tone for how a century of filmmakers would represent Lincoln in particular and the past in general on the screen. In that regard, the film's significance cannot be overestimated. Nor can the controversy that it caused.

Filming History

After a period of experimentation during which pioneering filmmakers explored ways to expand the new art of motion pictures, the emerging Hollywood studio system entered into its classical era. During this time the American cinema not only experienced a dramatic increase in popularity but also witnessed the emergence of a stylistic tendency that dominated film production for most of the twentieth century. The classical style "began quite early, in the period around 1909–1911, and . . . by 1917, the system was complete in its basic narrative and stylistic premises."[1] Experimental film forms continued to be produced by avant-garde filmmakers and independents working outside the growing studio system, but mainstream American movies quickly conformed to the classical style, which emphasized narrative content, continuity editing, and other elements now regarded as standard parts of the grammar of cinema.

Despite the ubiquity of the classical style, its defining feature was its invisibility. The goal was for each film "to conceal its artifice through techniques of continuity and 'invisible' storytelling."[2] For the typical fiction film, this meant that audiences were encouraged to suspend their disbelief and become immersed in the narrative. For the historical docudrama, however, the suspension of disbelief meant something quite different and far more consequential in that it directly influenced the perceived authenticity and historicity of the narrative. The film's form authenticates its content in ways that are rarely obvious to the casual viewer. Looking to be entertained, the viewer gets an education in historical causality that often flies under his or her critical radar.

Robert Brent Toplin explains that "cinematic historians have become powerful storytellers," noting that they "are competing effectively with the schoolteacher, the college professor, and the history book author."[3] Ultimately, the ideological power and potential of popular culture stems from its ability to "offer large numbers of people explanations of why things are the way things are—and what, if anything, can be done about it. Infuse this power with history—explanations of how things came to be the way they are—and you have a potent agent for influencing the thinking, and thus the actions, of millions of people."[4]

George F. Custen articulates an attitude about this power that is common among historians: "Hollywood biography is to history what Caesar's palace is to architectural history: an enormous, engaging distortion, which after a time convinces us of its own authenticity."[5] However, Robert A. Rosenstone, himself a historian, promotes a different perspective. Challenging traditional conceptions of history, he poses the following: "Isn't creating character and incident different from condensing events? Is it not destructive of history? Not history on film. On the screen history must be fictional in order to be true! . . . We must recognize that film will always include images that are at once invented and true; true in that they symbolize, condense, or summarize larger amounts of data; true in that they impart an overall meaning of the past that can be verified, documented, or reasonably argued."[6]

Even if one accepts the proposition that a film is neither superior nor inferior to a book in its inherent potential to create historical narrative, one must concede that the two do have obvious differences. Among these differences is the tendency of historical films shot in the classical style to render history "unknowable apart from its effects upon individual characters."[7] "Bad history is bad for culture," one historian cautions. "Americans need to know how change has occurred throughout history. . . . They need to understand the importance of institutions and organizations and movements."[8] In other words, assigning the causes to and illustrating the effects of historical events through the personal experiences of representative characters is a common, perhaps necessary, but unquestionably consequential narrative technique in classical Hollywood films.

Griffith's Masterpiece

"*The Birth of a Nation,*" one cultural critic notes, "represents two historical landmarks: an incomparable racial assault and a major breakthrough for subsequent filmmaking technique."[9] The two stories of D. W. Griffith's masterpiece—the story in the film and the story about the film—have received such extensive treatment that there is no real need to rehearse either yet again.[10] A cursory sketch of the film's production and reception will suffice as prelude to a concentrated look at the content and consequence of the film's depiction of Lincoln.

Lincoln appears in only a few brief scenes, but in many ways he serves as the character whose experience of the Civil War most effectively influences the viewer's understanding of that conflict. In addition, the film established a number of enduring precedents that continue to exert an almost incalculable influence over Lincoln's representation in other film and television productions. Indeed, *The Birth of a Nation* serves as the benchmark by which nearly all subsequent depictions of Lincoln have been measured. In spite of this, and in spite of all the attention this film as a whole has been given, its Lincoln remains largely unappreciated. The film's technical merits and blatant racism have obscured what might be its most important contribution: the creation of Hollywood's "Lincoln."

Hyperbole is not needed to suggest that *The Birth of a Nation* changed everything in the motion picture industry. This one silent film, released on the fiftieth anniversary of the end of the Civil War, forever changed how movies were both produced and consumed in America. Griffith's achievement lent "credence to motion pictures as an art form" and inspired a "revolution in American moviegoing."[11] Griffith was arguably already the most famous filmmaker in America during the silent era, Hollywood's "first auteur celebrity, its first star director."[12] He was not only famous, he was also quite good. His technical talent and narrative vision shaped America's sense of how stories were told, how past lives were remembered, and quite possibly how future lives would be lived. However, that is only part of his legacy. Griffith is remembered foremost as the man behind one of Hollywood's most controversial films.

David Llewelyn Wark Griffith was born in 1875 in La Grange, Kentucky, the son of a Confederate army officer and politician. He started his career as an actor and aspiring playwright, but in 1908 he began directing at the American Mutoscope and Biograph Company, where he made hundreds of short films. It was during this early phase of his directing career that Griffith experimented with the technical style—close-ups, crosscutting, and a moving camera, among other techniques—that later not only made him famous but also invented what is now called the classical Hollywood style. In fact, Griffith is closely associated not only with the Hollywood style but with Hollywood itself: his 1910 film, *In Old California,* is said to have been the first movie ever filmed in that now-iconic town that was then only a small, anonymous hamlet in Southern California.

Although he directed hundreds of films, Griffith's ambitious 190-minute Civil War epic is easily his most celebrated and successful. It is also his most notorious. *The Clansman,* later retitled *The Birth of a Nation,* was in 1915 an undeniable technical achievement, and its story structure changed the film industry as it evolved from pure visual spectacle toward a predominantly narrative cinema. The film is also sympathetic to the cause of the South to the point of celebrating the formation of the Ku Klux Klan, and it is so overtly racist in its portrayal of Reconstruction that former slaves are depicted as savage beasts suddenly set free on an otherwise civilized nation.

Racial and ethnic bigotry were as much a part of Griffith's films as the cinematic flair with which he directed them. His very first film, for example, was a one-reeler titled *The Adventures of Dollie* (1908) that demonstrated not only his potential but also "Griffith's narrow-mindedness, his distrust and dislike of immigrants and racial others."[13] The legacy of *The Birth of a Nation,* like that of Griffith's whole career, is similarly schizophrenic: his technical and narrative achievements positively changed the way movies were made, but the narrative content negatively changed the way Griffith would be remembered.

The Birth of a Nation was inspired by Thomas Dixon's novels *The Clansman* and, to a lesser extent, *The Leopard's Spots.* Like the nation it depicts, Griffith's film is divided in half, a structure that allowed for an intermission during lengthy theatrical screenings. Its plot is incredibly complex, especially for a film of this early era. The following summary omits most of the minor action because it is incidental to the present analysis of Lincoln's depiction.

Part 1 presents a peaceful and prosperous antebellum South that is disrupted and eventually destroyed by a war of Northern aggression. The seeds of disunion, however, are sown earlier, when the first Africans arrive in the United States. The struggle between North and South is symbolically represented in the form of a two-family drama with two love stories (the theme of doubles runs throughout the film). The Northern Stonemans and the Southern Camerons share little in common except for a childhood connection between their sons.

When the Stonemans visit the Cameron family on their South Carolina plantation, which Griffith's camera presents as an idyllic Eden before the fall, friendships are renewed among the sons and relationships are considered with the daughters.

But the outbreak of the war disrupts what is presented as a growing bond between North and South. Each family suffers casualties, but it is race and not region that causes the greatest suffering. The Cameron home is destroyed in the war not by Northern whites but by a black militia. As the war progresses, the bloodshed continues to be attributed to the contaminating presence of Africans in America. After much senseless violence, the war eventually ends. However, Lincoln's assassination is shown to make way for the cruel period of Reconstruction, wherein the North treats the well-being of former slaves as far more important than the welfare of white Southerners.

Part 2 depicts this agonizing process of Reconstruction. Angry with the South and emboldened by the loss of Lincoln, the North abandons the conciliatory posture of the Great Heart (as Lincoln is sometimes known for his determination to welcome the South back to the Union without punishment), adopting instead a punitive stance that favors the rights of freed slaves over those of Southern whites. As a necessary means of self-preservation, former Confederate soldiers form the Ku Klux Klan. The Klan is presented as a last line of defense, particularly for the women of the South, whose physical and moral safety are threatened by the new social order created by the war.

The film ends with the theme of duality once again punctuated, in this case with a double honeymoon. The Stonemans and the Camerons—still representing the North and the South—unite in not one but two marriages. Renewed unity is indeed possible, the film seems to suggest, but only if the South in general and the Klan in particular can succeed in controlling the "Negro threat."

Fifteen years after the release of his masterpiece, Griffith would try without success to jump-start his stalled career with a Lincoln biopic. Unlike *The Birth of a Nation, Abraham Lincoln* (1930) would prove to be a critical and financial failure, and it would seal Griffith's fate: the most talented filmmaker of the silent era would go into the history books as the artist who best gave voice to the very sentiments against which the Great Emancipator had fought and won.[14]

Shooting Lincoln

Although Lincoln is not the primary focus of *The Birth of a Nation*—far from it, in fact—the film's influence and legacy are so central to historical films in general, and to Lincoln films in particular, that one would be remiss not to examine his portrayal closely. Further, Lincoln's representation in the film remains something of a mystery despite all the attention given to the film. To the casual viewer, Lincoln's portrayal likely appears inconsequential. Yet if one examines the four major scenes in which he appears, and situates those scenes within the larger context of Lincoln's representations in American cinema throughout the twentieth and twenty-first centuries, it becomes clear that Griffith's Lincoln has greatly influenced several generations of filmmakers and audiences.

Lincoln first appears in *The Birth of a Nation* in a scene set in the president's office, where he is surrounded by officers and advisors. Lincoln (portrayed by Joseph Henabery) is shown agonizing over the decision to call for seventy-five thousand volunteers for the war. Urged on by those around him, Griffith's Lincoln is very much the reluctant warrior who, in the words of the historical Lincoln, "would accept war rather than let [the nation] perish." After signing the proclamation, Lincoln wipes his eyes and then interlaces his fingers in an ambiguous gesture that could simulate the act of praying.

The simple scene is significant for several reasons. First, it makes clear that of the many incarnations of Lincoln from which Griffith might have drawn, his Lincoln is to be foremost the Great Heart, in whom emotion and reason battle. Griffith's Lincoln is a tortured soul who agonizes over the war because even if the North wins, the South must therefore lose, and this Lincoln desires unity, not victory, and certainly not bloodshed among brothers. This representation is important because it allows Griffith to suggest that if not for Lincoln's assassination, the South would not have suffered as it did during Reconstruction. Ironically, from this perspective, it is Lincoln's tragic death that makes the formation of the Ku Klux Klan necessary. Finally, the first scene featuring Lincoln is accompanied by two intertitles. The second title card is pure ideology, lamenting that Lincoln would use the office of the presidency to restrict the rights of individual states. The first title card, however, is far more complicated.

The main text of the title card describes the moment in basic factual detail: "The First Call for 75,000 Volunteers. President Lincoln signing the proclamation." It is the footnote that accompanies the text, however, that is noteworthy in this analysis. In the bottom right corner of the screen are the words: "An historical facsimile of the President's Executive Office on that occasion, after Nicolay and Hay in 'Lincoln, A History.'" The presence of a footnote is not unique in this film, nor is it entirely unheard of in other historical movies of this era. Yet the impact of this one on the viewer's experience of Griffith's Lincoln is striking.

Early film audiences knew quite well the difference between what we now call documentary and docudrama, and thus there was no need to explain that the set is a facsimile—all the sets in the film are facsimiles—unless the intent is to suggest that what one is seeing might not be "real," but neither is it as "fake" as the typical historical film. Furthermore, by referencing Nicolay and Hay's nonfiction firsthand account of Lincoln's life and career,[15] Griffith furthers the cause of lobbying viewers to believe that what they are seeing possesses a greater authenticity than the typical movie about the past. The thrill of motion pictures always stemmed from their unique capacity to fool the eye, but *The Birth of a Nation* insists upon being regarded as occupying a space somewhere between docudrama and documentary, as existing in a state between reality and fiction—a state that I will define later in this chapter as *hyperreality.*

The extensive publicity for the film assured audiences that they would see "what really happened." The consequences of this appeal are many, but for the character of Lincoln it is clear that he was presented to audiences as what Umberto Eco calls an "absolute fake": a fabrication that is even better than the real thing, in this case because we are permitted an emotional access that would never have been possible with the real Lincoln but that is not only possible but encouraged with the hyperreal Lincoln.

The Pardon

Lincoln's second scene in the film is a familiar one, even for the viewer who has never seen *The Birth of a Nation*. The image of Lincoln pardoning a young soldier is ubiquitous, usually regarded as anticipating Lincoln's postwar attitude of reconciliation with the South. *The Blue and the Grey; or, the Days of '61* (1908), *Abraham Lincoln's Clemency* (1910), *The Sleeping Sentinel* (1910), *Grant and Lincoln* (1911), *The Romance of the '60s* (1911), *The Toll of War* (1913), *When Lincoln Paid* (1913), *When Lincoln Was President* (1913), *The Heart of Lincoln* (1915), *My Own United States* (1918), *The Highest Law* (1921), and *The Man without a Country* (1925) all feature Lincoln pardoning a young soldier, sometimes Union and sometimes Confederate, typically accused of treason, desertion, or falling asleep on duty.

By re-creating this scene more often than any other, Hollywood, like Washington, made his image as commander in chief paramount. By contrast, Lincoln's signing of the Emancipation Proclamation was not given extended attention until well into the twenty-first century. (It is nowhere mentioned in *The Birth of a Nation*.) *The Crisis* (1915) is a rare and notable exception. Almost certainly made to capitalize on the success of Griffith's *The Birth of a Nation,* this strikingly similar film focuses on a love story featuring a Northern soldier and a Southern belle. However, the film opens with a most unexpected scenario: Lincoln in front of a black background removing the shackles from a slave. The scene has been described as "completely divorced from the film's narrative, providing no context beyond simply presenting the image of Lincoln-as-emancipator."[16] Whatever the motivation, it remains a rare example of a film that assigns secondary status to Lincoln's role as Savior of the Union.

In Griffith's version of this enduring tale, the pardon involves the two families at the heart of the story, the Stonemans and the Camerons, and it is wrapped in two love stories. Colonel Ben Cameron is languishing in a Union army hospital being cared by for a nurse, Elsie Stoneman. Cameron has loved her since he saw her picture before the war when his old schoolmate, Phil Stoneman, visited his family. Just as Mrs. Cameron arrives to visit her ailing son, it is announced that he is to be hanged. The two women devise a plan to save him; they will ask for mercy from "the Great Heart."

Precisely how the women earn an audience with the president is not clear. After first appearing to decline to intervene, Lincoln eventually agrees to pardon Colonel Cameron. Back in the hospital, the Confederate officer is told by his mother: "Mr. Lincoln has given your life back to me." The soldier is symbolic of the South as a whole, which this Lincoln intended to welcome back into the Union like a prodigal son.

Lincoln's third appearance is little more than a continuation of his second scene. Instead of a mother from the South pleading with Lincoln to show mercy, Griffith delivers a father from the North pleading for Lincoln to show no mercy. After Lee's surrender to Grant at Appomattox Courthouse, Austin Stoneman urges the president to execute the leaders of the Confederate army as an example to the South and to treat the Southern states like conquered nations. To Stoneman's frustration, Lincoln refuses to take such revenge, promising instead to welcome back the Southern states "as though they had never been away." These two scenes are early examples of one of Hollywood's most common characterizations of Abraham Lincoln: the Great Heart who balanced reason with emotion for the good of both the individual and the nation as a whole.

These two scenes are also responsible for what may be the most interesting interpretation of Griffith's Lincoln: as an androgynous or feminine character.[17] Precisely how critics of the film have found in these scenes evidence to support an interpretation involving gender or sexuality is not entirely clear, but most point to the emotional agony that Lincoln demonstrates during the war, especially the moment in which he pulls a shawl up over his shoulders. One such critic describes the scene as "totally out of character for the real Lincoln, who by many contemporary accounts disliked publicly displaying great emotion or sentiment."[18]

Be that as it may, an anguished Lincoln looking to God for guidance became a standard incarnation in the cinema. One could just as easily read this moment as a silent film's melodramatic means of expressing Lincoln's state of mind which, according to Griffith, is largely sympathetic to the South, as well as a foreshadowing of what's to come for Lincoln. However, even if such a reading is not textually warranted, enough critics have read ambiguous sexuality into these scenes that it has become a part of the film's legacy.

Martyrdom

The assassination sequence, Lincoln's fourth and final appearance, is the longest and most significant in the entire film. It is not the content of the sequence that is so important, but rather the manner in which that content is contextualized. The assassination is the last sequence and thus the dramatic culmination of the first part of this two-part film. The sequence is elaborate, rivaling even the complicated and impressive battle scenes for which the film has been celebrated. According to one source, Griffith's elaborate staging of Lincoln's assassination includes fifty-five individual shots, nine intertitles, and lasts for roughly five minutes of screen time.[19] The staging of the assassination sequence played to and benefited from this overall aura of authenticity.

The sequence begins with a title card that locates the narrative in time and place. Most important, it includes a footnote: "An historical facsimile of Ford's Theater as on that night, exact in size and detail, with the recorded incidents, after Nicolay and Hay in 'Lincoln, A History.'" The scholarly footnote lends credibility to the visual content, creating the impression that the scene has more in common with a thoroughly researched museum exhibit than a typical Hollywood movie set. The next shot reveals Griffith's impressive facsimile: Ford's Theatre is unveiled through a slowly opening iris that reveals its amazing size and impressive detail. When the president and his party arrive, they are greeted with a standing ovation. What follows is familiar to us all: the play begins, Booth slips into the presidential box, discharges his weapon, and leaps to the stage where he shouts, "Sic semper tyrannis!" Chaos ensues in the audience—and across the country.

Thematically, the sequence represents the intersection of Griffith's dual genres: the family melodrama (members of the Stoneman family are present in the theater) and the historical biopic of Lincoln. Historically, the significance of the sequence is obvious. A century after the film's release, it remains the definitive visualization of the murder of Abraham Lincoln. We have no photographs of Lincoln from that fateful night, and of course motion picture technology did not yet exist. For the Kennedy assassination, we have Abraham Zapruder's footage. For the Reagan assassination attempt, we have video from news cameras. For the Lincoln assassination, we have Griffith's *The Birth of a Nation.*

And this is where the film's real cultural power rests. It is here in Ford's Theatre where fiction and nonfiction meet, where reality and make-believe mingle and blur. The film's ability to position itself somewhere between documentary and docudrama is due in large part to its self-professed level of historical accuracy, especially in the assassination sequence. But if the film's apparent authenticity is impressive, even that pales in comparison to the legendary efforts put forth by Griffith and his studio to advertise the film's authenticity, especially the scene of Lincoln's murder. Indeed, the film in general and the assassination in particular were heavily advertised as something akin to a living history event. Even the decision to change the name of the film from *The Clansman* to *The Birth of a Nation* was part of an unprecedented marketing campaign designed not only to deflect criticism of a controversial take on (what was in 1915) recent American history but also to persuade audiences that this film would fulfill the promise of motion pictures by providing the audience with a clear view of "what really happened."

Convincing viewers that they would experience reality in a space that by 1915 was already synonymous with fantasy required "a deeply imaginative array of stunts and promotional devices" that "pioneered most of the major methods that would later be used by the Hollywood studios and their chains of theaters to 'sell' moving pictures."[20] These included several bold claims, among them the boasts that the film was the biggest ever staged, the most expensive ever produced, and the most patriotic ever imagined. Most important was the central claim regarding the film's value as a part of history. Theater ushers wore authentic blue and gray Civil War uniforms, intertitles attested to the film's exhaustive research, and screenings were treated like monumental events: at the two hundredth screening, for example, audience members were given souvenir programs. It was as if the fiftieth anniversary of the end of the Civil War was being overshadowed by "anniversaries" of the film about the Civil War. Griffith had not simply adhered to the historical record (at least according to the promotional material), his film had apparently become part of it.

Hyperreality

The apparently intentional collapse of presenting history and making history afforded Griffith's film an aura of hyperrealism never before enjoyed by a motion picture. Hyperreality is a concept explained by no single definition. For the purposes of this chapter, however, the following will suffice: hyperreality "signifies a rupture in the notion of the real brought on by techniques of mass reproduction."[21]

The term *hyperreality* has been used primarily by scholars in the field of semiotics, most prominently by Umberto Eco and Jean Baudrillard, to refer to a range of phenomena in modern, technological, mass-mediated societies—phenomena in which it is difficult to separate the real from representations of the real. The two scholars use the term in similar but not identical ways: "Both Eco and Baudrillard have identified American pop culture as a form of hyperreality . . . yet whereas Eco defines the hyperreality of America as consisting of artificial copies of authentic originals . . . Baudrillard sees America as the ultimate simulacrum, no longer an artificial copy of an authentic original but an endless chain of copies referring to each other."[22] Indeed, Baudrillard argues that we have lost entirely our ability to experience reality, that all that is available to us is a copy world filled with simulations of the real. As he famously observed, "Illusion is no longer possible, because the real is no longer possible."[23] Baudrillard's explanation likely better describes the experience a viewer has watching a Lincoln film in the twenty-first century—a film whose creator is copying other fictional Lincolns depicted in earlier Lincoln films.

Of course, such was not the case for Griffith and his audience. In 1915, audiences knew Lincoln as a recent public figure, not a name from the distant past or the embodiment of a set of abstract principles. When that point is combined with the newness of motion pictures, it is clear that these viewers related to Griffith's Lincoln in a way that future audiences would not and could not do. For his audience, Griffith's Lincoln was a bridge between history and cinema—a gap they could cross given their connection to Lincoln in his own lifetime.

Umberto Eco once traveled across the United States visiting tourist destinations in which the fake is offered not merely as a substitute for the real but as an improvement upon it. In his landmark book, *Travels in Hyperreality,* Eco describes visiting a German castle in Disneyland, Egyptian pyramids in Las Vegas, celebrities in various houses of wax, and "wild" animals in unnatural habitats (zoos). "The American imagination demands the real thing," he wrote, "and, to attain it, must fabricate the absolute fake."[24]

Griffith's goal was to lure audiences to theaters and thus maximize profits, but his very successful economic strategy had perhaps unintended social and political consequences. Among them was the generation of the sense that Griffith had used film to capture the *real* Lincoln. This changed the way audiences perceived not only Lincoln—whose image would be shaped far more significantly in Griffith's 1930 Lincoln biopic—but also how they perceived motion pictures and their relation to the past. Griffith had indeed made history, not merely by directing a film of unprecedented success but by changing the way people felt about what they experienced in the cinema.

The literature on Griffith and *The Birth of a Nation* is not silent on the matter of Lincoln's representation. Still, most critics have addressed the Lincoln character only in passing, apparently regarding him as only a bit player in this grand historical epic. Although Lincoln's portrayal in the film may seem unremarkable within the confines of this single text, it is important that we recognize it in the larger context of future Lincoln films. The Lincoln one finds in *The Birth of a Nation* greatly influenced other filmmakers who later brought Lincoln to the screen. Admittedly, Griffith did not explore the image or shape the memory of Lincoln in this film as much as he might have done. However, his choices were not without consequence, as he established the cinematic style and narrative scenarios within which Lincoln would be endlessly situated.

In addition to the enormous influence over filmmakers that we may rightly attribute to the Lincoln in Griffith's *The Birth of a Nation,* we must also recognize its effect on film theory. Griffith carefully and cleverly situated Lincoln in a space between reality and fiction. Griffith did so, it seems safe to assume, as part of a successful marketing campaign designed to advertise his film as the most historically accurate ever made. However, even if Griffith's intentions were purely economic, his actions had substantial artistic and intellectual consequences. His 1915 Lincoln is a classic—perhaps *the* classic—example of what Eco called the absolute fake: an artificial copy of an original that is so perfect that the representation of the real has in many ways replaced the real within our minds.

Reflecting on the power of Lincoln's oratory, the historian Garry Wills once said, "The Civil War *is,* to most people, what Lincoln wanted it to *mean.* Words had to complete the work of the guns."[25] Lincoln's words may have advanced the work of the guns, but Griffith's images completed it. His interpretation of the Civil War and Reconstruction has not been adopted and is uniformly regarded as biased and racist. Still, when we imagine the war in general and Lincoln's death in particular, it is footage from *The Birth of a Nation* that we see in our mind's eye. And that is Griffith's powerful and invisible legacy.

3

Savior of the Union

Abraham Lincoln (1930)

> *Abraham Lincoln* was surely the first major historical film of the sound era, a beginning of an attempt to reclaim the past for the movies.
> —Richard Schickel, *D. W. Griffith: An American Life*

Stephen Vincent Benét had just won the 1929 Pulitzer Prize for poetry for his book-length narrative poem *John Brown's Body* when D. W. Griffith asked him to write a screenplay for *Abraham Lincoln* (1930). Like many successful writers in the early twentieth century, Benét made the trek to Hollywood with no small sense of apprehension. As it turned out, he had reason to be skeptical about the promise of "the pictures." By the time filming wrapped on his first project, Benét was so disillusioned with Hollywood that he fled the film industry forever. Benét would go on to write, among other literary classics, the famous short story "The Devil and Daniel Webster," about a man who sold his soul to Satan. There is no direct evidence that the tale was inspired by Benét's time in Hollywood, but it's within the realm of reason. In a letter to his agent, Benét wrote of the dream factory: "I don't know which makes me vomit worst—the horned toads from the cloak and suit trade, the shanty Irish, or the gentlemen who talk of Screen Art."[1]

If Benét's star was on the rise in the late 1920s, D. W. Griffith's was falling fast. He had once been the most famous filmmaker in Hollywood, but his career had faltered, and Griffith was hoping that a second look at Lincoln might give him a second chance in the movies. It was not to be. The filming of *Abraham Lincoln* was so difficult and its reception so lukewarm that Griffith actually accused the studio, United Artists, of deliberately sabotaging the production to justify getting rid of him. Claims of a conspiracy are unsupported, but the film did indeed end Griffith's career.

How Abraham Lincoln fared amid the drama that plagued the production of his first full-length biopic of the sound era is not yet fully understood. Although the timing of the production was perfect—it enjoyed a wide release just as America's fascination with Lincoln was peaking—*Abraham Lincoln* has come to occupy an uncertain place in the history of U.S. popular culture. The film received limited critical praise, but it was not a financial success, and history has concentrated on how the film drove Benét out of Hollywood and Griffith out of the movies, largely ignoring its impact on the memory and evolving image of Abraham Lincoln.

The oversight is unfortunate. *Abraham Lincoln* is a complex and fascinating film, one that critics ignore at the cost of a deeper understanding of Lincoln's place in our national memory. Griffith's first "talkie" chronicles Lincoln's life in full: from his birth in a Kentucky log cabin to his assassination at Ford's Theatre in Washington, D.C. The first major historical picture of the sound era, it offers an episodic mixture of historic milestones and anecdotal asides. In this chapter, I demonstrate that Griffith's biopic depicts Lincoln as the Savior of the Union with such singular determination that all other dimensions of his character and career are either drastically minimized or entirely ignored. Had anyone other than Griffith directed the film, it might be possible to dismiss its obsessive focus on Lincoln as a war president as little more than an artistic choice—which it may well have been. However, given the overt racism in several of Griffith's other films, especially *The Birth of a Nation,* it was possible then, and remains possible now, to read the film differently.

By accident or design, *Abraham Lincoln* resonates with an early twentieth-century struggle over which of Lincoln's many incarnations would dominate the American mind. The war to interpret Lincoln had been raging since his death, but with the design of the Lincoln Memorial a major victory had recently been won for those wanting to obscure Lincoln's connection to the question of race and the problem of slavery. Griffith's film, like the memorial itself, concentrates on the image of the Savior of the Union and ignores almost entirely the representation of Lincoln as the

Great Emancipator. Together, both texts performed consequential memory work, altering the way a generation of Americans remembered its collective past and defined itself in relation to Abraham Lincoln.

Carl Sandburg

At the peak of his career, D. W. Griffith was an important man in America. He maintained a "lively correspondence" with the likes of Woodrow Wilson and William Jennings Bryan, and his films twice received special showings at the White House.[2] The boy born in 1875 in rural Kentucky had come a long way from his impoverished youth. Of his childhood, Griffith wrote in an unfinished autobiography: "Make no mistake, I hold no nostalgic grief for the past. Edison, Ford, and Marconi were still dreams back in those days . . . so were the plumbers."[3] It was from those early days that Griffith drew inspiration for *The Birth of a Nation:* "One could not find the sufferings of our family and our friends—the dreadful poverty and hardships during the war and for many years after—in the Yankee-written histories we read in school. From all this was born a burning determination to tell some day our side of the story to the world."[4]

That the son of a slave-owning veteran of the Confederate cause would one day choose to film the life of the Savior of the Union must have been a surprise to some who knew him in his youth. However, in an attempt to energize a once-illustrious career that had faltered after synchronized sound had been introduced into the industry that he had built, Griffith decided that it was time to make another historical drama. When studio executives expressed doubt about the public's interest in the project he initially proposed—a film version of Benét's epic *John Brown's Body*—Griffith decided that a film about Abraham Lincoln surely would enjoy universal appeal. What followed was an ordeal that Griffith would later describe as "a nightmare of the mind and nerves."[5]

Determined to make a successful picture about Lincoln, Griffith offered a job as historical consultant to Carl Sandburg, the Pulitzer Prize-winning writer best known for his popular biographies *Abraham Lincoln: The Prairie Years* and *Abraham Lincoln: The War Years.* Sandburg, whom Edmund Wilson once described as "the worst thing to happen to Lincoln since Booth shot him," was so enthusiastic about the idea that he volunteered to reschedule several other projects in order to play a more significant role in developing the film.[6] In a telegram to Griffith on October 13, 1929, Sandburg wrote: "Keenly interested in seeing Lincoln picture done which will be a series of personality sketches setting forth his tremendous range of tragic and comic. . . . Know almost precisely what is wanted for historical accuracy woven with dramatic interest. . . . All past presentations have faked hokum while neglecting established and entertaining dramatic values of Lincoln."[7]

Despite Sandburg's enthusiasm, the collaboration never materialized. Sandburg was allegedly unwilling to work for less than $30,000, which Griffith was unable to offer, and the film was made without the writer's direct assistance. Still, Sandburg's indirect influence is undeniable. Griffith most assuredly had read Sandburg's volumes on Lincoln, and ultimately the filmmaker "would follow Sandburg's advice; his *Abraham Lincoln* would be a highly episodic work, alternating anecdotal incident and great historic moments."[8]

The Players

Sandburg was eventually replaced by Benét, who arrived in Hollywood during what one historian has called the film industry's "most irresponsible and unstable era." "The conversion to sound had brought staggering profits and the destructive knowledge that the most trivial material would be richly rewarded at the box office."[9] It was immediately clear to Benét that he was well out of his element in Southern California. In one of a series of fascinating letters he sent to his wife, Rosemary, Benét confessed, "My script is full of things like 'Camera trucks, shooting from reverse angle.' They sound fine, but I don't know what any of them mean."[10]

The poet penned countless rewrites of John Considine's script for continually unsatisfied studio executives, including one version that Benét claimed contained "every historical character & incident in it except Millard Fillmore repairing the White House plumbing."[11] Another version mixed major events of Lincoln's life with a love story involving a young woman and a Union soldier. When, near the conclusion of the film, audiences were to find "the old chestnut of Lincoln pardoning a young soldier," both plot lines would have come together and audiences would have realized the impact Lincoln had on so many individual lives.[12] In the words of one critic, this device "would have given a plotless film a plot."[13] But the romance was cut from the final script; it was a decision that Griffith would come to regret. "Lincoln, after all, could furnish little suspense," Griffith later conceded. "The audience already knows what is going to happen to him."[14]

One biographer credits this decision and others equally unwise to "Griffith's drinking, described, even by himself, as an illness; his sense of insecurity; and his inability to keep from 'improving' the work of others with sycophantic, but inept, assistance."[15] Others contend that much malice was involved in the treatment Griffith was receiving from executives at United Artists. "Whether consciously or not, [United Artists' producer Joseph] Schenck and his henchmen might have decided that if he could not be gotten rid of cleanly, a dirty job would do—by politely sabotaging his last-chance production."[16] Whatever the cause, even Griffith lamented that the final version of the film contained too many facts and not enough fun.

As for Benét, he was impressed with Griffith. In another letter to his wife, Benét wrote, "The work goes on. I think we're about through & then Mr. Griffith has a new idea. The trouble is—he's generally perfectly right. I continue to like him."[17] Benét's assessment of the industry as a whole was not so favorable. In a letter to Carl Brandt, his literary agent, Benét wrote:

> I have worked in advertising and with W. A. Brady Sr. But nowhere have I seen such shining waste, stupidity and conceit as in the business and managing end of this industry. Whoopee!
>
> Since arriving, I have written 4 versions of *Abraham Lincoln,* including a good one, playable in their required time. That, of course, is out. Seven people, including myself, are now working in conferences on the 5th one, which promises hopefully to be the worst yet. If I don't get out of here soon I'm going to go crazy. Perhaps I am crazy now. I wouldn't be surprised.
>
> At any rate, don't be surprised if you get a wire from me that I

> have broken my contract, bombed the studio, or been arrested for public gibbering. Don't be surprised at all.[18]

It came as no surprise to Griffith when Benét declined his offer to collaborate on a future film about the Alamo. In fact, as soon as shooting on *Abraham Lincoln* began, Benét left Hollywood and never returned. Griffith seemed to have enjoyed working with Benét, but his final thoughts on *Abraham Lincoln* reduced the experience to a cliché: "Too many cooks spoil the broth."[19]

The studio eventually settled on Walter Huston to play the role of Lincoln, based largely on the recommendation of George M. Cohan, the legendary Broadway composer, actor, playwright and producer. After, the eight-week shoot, Griffith retreated to Mineral Wells, Texas, leaving the filming of special effects and the crucial editing process to others at United Artists. It was an uncharacteristic and ultimately unwise decision. When his requests for changes to the final cut were refused, Griffith and the studio agreed to part ways and to forego the next film that he was already under contract to make. It was the end for Griffith.

The Critics

Although *Abraham Lincoln* was not a commercial success, the critics were kind. The *New York Times* voted it one of the ten best films of 1930. The following year, the Motion Picture Academy of Arts and Sciences named Griffith "Director of the Year," as did *Film Daily* and *New Movie Magazine.* Early reviewers seem to have satisfied themselves by celebrating the subject of Lincoln, and then forcing the film on audiences as something close to a patriotic duty. One critic, apparently intoxicated by what he had just seen, declared: "More than an outstanding classic of sound pictures, *Abraham Lincoln* . . . is a startlingly superlative accomplishment; one rejuvenating a greatest Griffith. In characterization and detail perfection is such as to be almost unbelievable. In continuity and scenes it projects as one smooth roll of literally throbbing pulsation, pathos, laughter, with never a moment's interlude for audience let-down."[20]

Thus the first major historical film of the era of synchronized sound was indeed an initial critical success, but over the years even the critics have turned on Griffith's first talkie. Richard Schickel offers one possible explanation for this dramatic turning of the tide.

> It is . . . odd that the picture's reputation has suffered a decline in recent years, particularly among Griffith specialists. Perhaps because of a desire to rescue his next and final film, *The Struggle,* from the calumnies heaped upon it, there is a need to make invidious comparisons between it and its immediate predecessor, as well as a need to prove that in this period contemporary critics were suddenly struck blind on the subject of Griffith. But if *Abraham Lincoln* is no masterpiece, it is also quite an engaging film; and considering what talking pictures had been up until that moment, one can easily understand why contemporary critics were so taken with its pictorialism, its moments of near lyricism.[21]

Whatever the reason, the years have not been kind to *Abraham Lincoln.* The historian Merrill D. Peterson argues: "Actor and director tried to capture the sad and poetic young Lincoln, but the screen portrait is wooden, sentimental, and stale. It is Sandburg without grace or humor."[22] At the heart of the debate regarding the film's artistry is its noticeably episodic structure, consisting almost entirely of well-known moments from Lincoln's life. Conventional wisdom holds that this approach was a mistake. "Only through new insights into Lincoln's character and his relationships with his family and loves," argues one critic, "might the audience's interest have been stimulated. . . . Animated history is not drama no matter how worthy the subject."[23] Another suggests that the film "might, in fact, have been called something like *Beloved Moments with Mr. Lincoln,* as it was essentially a compilation of the most familiar 'humanizing' anecdotes about him—the stuff of schoolbook histories—and inescapable historical highlights."[24]

Not everyone looks back on *Abraham Lincoln* with such derision. Andrew Sarris, who revolutionized film scholarship in 1968 with his publication of *The American Cinema,* sees the film quite differently. "Very early in his career [Griffith] mastered most of the technical vocabulary of the cinema and then proceeded to simplify his vocabulary for the sake of greater psychological penetration of the dramatic issues that concerned him. Hence, what seemed like a precipitous decline in the early thirties with *Abraham Lincoln* (1930) . . . was in reality a precious distillation of what had been achieved in earlier films."[25] Still, Sarris is firmly in the minority. Despite the initial accolades that *Abraham Lincoln* afforded him, Griffith made only one other film (*The Struggle,* 1931), which generally is considered his worst.

The historical community has been especially harsh on this and other Lincoln films. Merrill Peterson contends that most of Hollywood's Lincoln films succeed in capturing only "the shadow of Lincoln rather than the substance, the templed god rather than the historic figure, the spiritual legacy of the words rather than the life, that mattered."[26] Don E. Fehrenbacher charges that fictional presentations of Lincoln are typically "a blend not only of historical fact and literary invention but of folklore and myth—especially the folklore of the American west and the myth of the dying god."[27] David Donald, the Pulitzer Prize-winning Lincoln biographer, finds that artistic accounts of Lincoln's life too often result in a "portrait [that] looks somewhat like a Gilbert Stuart painting with a halo dubbed in by later, less skillful hands."[28]

Whether the professional historian is in the best position to judge an artistic representation is a matter of debate, but there is no question that the historical community finds most Lincoln films, including and perhaps especially Griffith's *Abraham Lincoln,* to be unworthy of their subject.

The Savior

The goal of this analysis is to understand the film's presentation of Lincoln as an interpretive argument, one that advances a very particular characterization of Lincoln and of the Civil War. *Abraham Lincoln* tells the tale of a savior's birth, life, death, and rebirth. This depiction is underscored by Lincoln's mantra—"The Union must be preserved!"—which he utters in slightly varying forms in no fewer than seven separate scenes.

Hodgenville

Abraham Lincoln opens with an extended credit sequence during which the screen is framed with trees. The title "Abraham Lincoln" is written in a script that resembles logs or tree branches. In the first frame, Griffith's name appears as large as Lincoln's, and a subsequent frame assures viewers that Griffith "personally" directed the film. Behind Griffith's credit appears the image of a log cabin, again uniting director and subject. A medley of Civil War-era music accompanies the entire credit sequence and reminds viewers how Lincoln's story, which has not yet begun, eventually will end.

The structure of this first section of the film is highly episodic, but unlike subsequent sections it is marked by an invisible style similar to most of early Hollywood's biographical films. The narrative begins with a tracking shot of a dark forest, likely shot in miniature. As strong winds blow and wolves or coyotes howl, viewers are moved through the forest to a secluded cabin. Coinciding with an impressive dissolve from the miniature log cabin to one in actual size is the appearance of the title: "February 12, 1809." Outside the cabin a middle-aged man who is chopping wood is told that his wife is giving birth, but that "'taint far enough along yet fer a tag."

The following scene takes us inside the cabin, by which time the infant boy already has been born. Unlike in literary biographies, birth scenes are not common in biographical films. Of the major Lincoln films analyzed in this book, only *Abraham Lincoln* chronicles Lincoln's entire life. George F. Custen found that of the one hundred biographical films in his representative sample, only three took audiences all the way from the cradle to the grave. "The absence of the full life," Custen admits, "is puzzling."[29] But by beginning in medias res, biopics are able to imply that their subjects have invented themselves. The technique of concealing a character's origin creates "a picture of history as a narrative of powerful individuals, who, by dint of remarkable gifts, are able to override conventional definitions of a social reality held by a restrictive community. That is, the great man can literally write—or rewrite—history."[30] But Lincoln is different; his life seems both self-made and divinely intended. To reconcile that apparent contradiction *Abraham Lincoln* presents Lincoln's birth but conceals his childhood.

All of the predictable elements are there in *Abraham Lincoln*'s next scene: the midwife jokes that the boy is "homely," and a child predicts, "Shucks, he'll never amount to nuthin,' no how!" Such remarks provide an important element of the biopic: "an early—and formidable—example of adversity to be surmounted."[31] However, the dying utterance of Lincoln's mother, Nancy ("Abraham!") is delivered with such drama, such reverence, that it seems that in naming the boy a prophecy is fulfilled.

New Salem

The next sequence begins with a clumsy relic of the silent cinema that helps to conceal Lincoln's childhood: an hourglass is shown, along with the words, "The story of a man begins." The film cuts to a sign shown in close-up that reads, "D. Offut Proprietor, Abraham Lincoln Clerk." It is now approximately 1832, and Lincoln is a young man in his early twenties who has moved away from home to the town of New Salem, Illinois, where he is employed as a store clerk. The leap in time, signified by the hourglass, is significant. Lincoln's birth, which is presented with such drama, attests to the monumental significance of his life. However, viewers are quickly swept away from his family and formative years. As a consequence, Lincoln's character and values are shown not as the result of his upbringing, which is absent, but rather are already in place when viewers first meet him as a young man. Thus Lincoln's birth seems prophetic while his character seems to be of his own making.

The New Salem sequence is drawn in part from Sandburg's *Prairie Years*, and it is a staple in many Lincoln films. Offut, speaking as much for the film's viewers as to the anonymous customer in the store, says, "There he is—ugliest, laziest, smartest man in New Salem." Sprawled across the counter and holding a book, as he is almost always shown in films that depict his New Salem years, Lincoln offers a humorous and self-deprecating reply. Then, after being told that New Salem is not a "peaceable town," to which he replies that he is a "peaceable man," Lincoln is accosted by Jack Armstrong, a minor character who often appears in written accounts of

Lincoln's early life. The fight carries over into the street and, to the delight of the entire citizenry, Lincoln triumphs. Afterward, he declares, "I'm the big buck in this lick!"[32] The men head back into the general store and all but Lincoln begin drinking. After amazing his new friends with his ability to lift an entire barrel of beer, Lincoln tells them, "I don't regulate no one's drinkin'—just my own."

The following scene features Lincoln splitting rails as Ann Rutledge reads aloud from a book on law—probably Blackstone's *Commentaries*, which the historical Lincoln is thought to have read while in New Salem. Griffith's Lincoln is here surprisingly flirtatious, but his relationship with Rutledge functions to humanize him for the audience in ways otherwise not possible. Soon "Uncle Jimmy" rides by on a horse-drawn wagon and tells Rutledge that Lincoln is "the best rail-splitter in the country." She replies, "He'll be more than a rail-splitter!" Utilizing a technique common among biographical films, Lincoln's friends and associates (Offut, Rutledge, Uncle Jimmy, and later William Herndon and Mary Todd) function as character witnesses testifying on Lincoln's behalf before the film's viewers. Each of these characters acts as "a guide to the audience, getting us to empathize with these great figures, but also to revere them."[33]

The film next moves on to an event that likely never occurred in the life of the historical Lincoln: a proposal of marriage to Ann Rutledge. Lincoln's relationship with Rutledge, although historically suspect, is another staple in Hollywood's versions of his life. Their romance almost always functions as an early tragedy from which Lincoln draws the strength needed to endure future hardships. *Abraham Lincoln*, however, may be the only Lincoln film to include an explicit proposal and acceptance of marriage. Griffith's motivation for taking such license becomes clear immediately: only a commitment of this intensity could serve as *the* formative and catalyzing experience in Lincoln's early life. The loss of a lover to whom one is not entirely devoted might not realistically figure as the definitive turning point in a narrative. As the scene closes, Lincoln tells his love, "I feel as though I'm going to be seeing your face until the day I die." Audiences now understand that Rutledge's impending death will haunt Lincoln until his own.

Until now Lincoln has appeared amiable and relatively happy, even when fighting Armstrong. However, it is a somber Lincoln who arrives at the Rutledge home to learn that his fiancée is dying. The moment is significant because it reinforces the theme of death that was introduced immediately following Lincoln's birth. Although Lincoln's attention is devoted fully to Rutledge, our thoughts seem directed by their dialogue toward Lincoln's own inevitable demise. "It's so dark and lonesome," Rutledge mutters. "If they'd sing I wouldn't be so afraid." An angelic chorus swells on the soundtrack as a dying Rutledge adds, "We will meet there, dear." A slow fade to black gives the audience sufficient time to contemplate Lincoln's death.

The scene following Rutledge's death is remarkable; it may feature the most emotionally distraught image of Lincoln ever filmed. Stumbling about a cabin occupied by a middle-aged couple of unspecified relation, Lincoln appears in a trancelike state as he recites lines from Keats's poem "On Death." His knife, we learn, has been taken from him as a precaution. Eventually Lincoln finds his way outside in the midst of a raging storm (similar to the evening of his mother's death), he throws himself on Rutledge's grave, and sobs uncontrollably.

Springfield

We next encounter Lincoln as he arrives on horseback in Springfield, Illinois. His first official action is to dismount his horse and surrender it to the sheriff to pay off a debt. Honest Abe has arrived. We are introduced to Mary Todd, who talks with her sister about Stephen A. Douglas and Abraham Lincoln—the two men she is considering for marriage. We soon find Lincoln and Douglas already in competition, sparring for Todd's attention at a party.

The following scenes are important stylistically because they comprise one of only two instances in the entire film of crosscutting between simultaneous actions. The opening Springfield sequence begins in the same way the New Salem sequence did: with a close-up of a sign outside Lincoln's new place of employment. It reads: "Stuart and Lincoln, Attorneys at Law." Inside, Lincoln reveals to William Herndon his doubts about marrying Mary Todd. Next, Todd is shown as she prepares for the wedding. Lincoln, now alone in the law office, looks at a picture of Ann Rutledge and calls out her name. Todd is next shown dismissing the wedding guests as she realizes that Lincoln has left her at the altar. The unusual sequence ends when Lincoln finally arrives, without explanation, and commits to marrying Mary Todd.

The structure of the film up to this point is interesting because only in hindsight is one able to recognize that a particular pattern of events is repeated. Historically, a span of nearly a year separated Lincoln and Todd's first wedding date from the date of their eventual marriage, but *Abraham Lincoln* makes no attempt to account for that lost time. What seems to matter more than the historical details is Griffith's ability to create a narrative pattern that suggests causality. The pattern is fairly simple: Lincoln experiences the loss of a woman he loves (Nancy Lincoln/Ann Rutledge), time passes, Lincoln moves to a new town (New Salem/Springfield), he begins a new job (store clerk/lawyer), and eventually enters into a romantic relationship (Ann Rutledge/Mary Todd).

The cyclical pattern is a familiar one in the genre of the biopic, and it is followed almost exactly in the opening scenes of John Cromwell's 1940 film, *Abe Lincoln in Illinois*. In this case, however, the effect that this pattern of loss has had on Lincoln, and on the audience, is quite clear. In the future, Lincoln will work tirelessly to prevent similarly devastating losses—a commitment that will take shape most clearly in Lincoln's repeated proclamations that "the Union must be preserved!"

This theme is introduced explicitly in an interesting montage that purports to feature scenes of the Lincoln-Douglas debates. What is most remarkable about Griffith's re-creation of the debates is that the montage would have the viewer believe that these legendary debates were concerned primarily with the possibility of Southern secession. In fact, the real debates focused almost entirely on matters pertaining to slavery.[34] The shift is significant, not merely because it is a blatant example of historical revisionism but because here Lincoln is positioned to be the future Savior of the Union, not the Great Emancipator, even before he arrives in Washington. The montage of the debates, although brief, shapes the lens through which we see Lincoln's presidency, which occupies almost half the film. In this biopic, Lincoln was born to save the Union—not free the slaves.

Washington, D.C.

After moving into the White House, an experience that prompts endless complaining from Mrs. Lincoln, all thoughts turn to the war that the audience knows is soon to come. Griffith's staging of the conflict will occupy much of the rest of the film. The war is heralded by an on-screen title: "Fort Sumter. 4:30 A.M. April 12, 1861. Confederate guns open fire and Civil War begins." The scene marks only the second time that the narrative has been anchored to an exact date (the first was Lincoln's birth, February 12, 1809).

The war is presented by Griffith in a manner quite unlike all that has preceded it. Gone are the subtle use of repetitive structuring and the not-so-subtle use of characters who act as witnesses testifying before the audience on Lincoln's behalf. In place of these techniques is a simple event-by-event account of Lincoln's agonizing experience during the Civil War. After a melodramatic scene in which soldiers of both armies march off to war, the narrative turns to Lincoln as he waits with more patience than most viewers for repeated updates on the fighting. Although the film's few battle scenes have been praised for their realism, they are little more than spectacle. The pace and mood of the narrative slow dramatically during the war as a result of Griffith's decision to focus on Lincoln and not the fighting. The decision is understandable—after all, the film is first and foremost about Abraham Lincoln, and Griffith had already made his sweeping Civil War epic a decade and a half earlier.

In place of the action that additional battle scenes would have afforded, Griffith offers a penetrating look at the psychological effect the war is having on Lincoln. A subtle change does occur within this section, however, regarding the audience's knowledge of specific information. At first viewers must wait until Lincoln has received word from the telegraph office before they are told through Lincoln of the status of the fighting. For instance, the Union soldiers' retreat to Washington is shown only after Lincoln announces that the South is winning and that the capital must be defended. However, later in the film viewers are permitted to observe the progress of the war before Lincoln hears of it, and thus the drama centers around Lincoln's reaction to the news. One consequence of this transition from drama to dramatic irony is an even greater emphasis on Lincoln rather than the war. What results is a chronicle of the agonizingly deliberate process of presidential decision making during wartime as it had never before been portrayed on film.

The scene featuring the president pardoning a young Union soldier (the most common in Lincoln's extensive filmography) was originally intended to unite the primary drama (the war) with Benét's proposed subplot (the romance between a soldier and his childhood sweetheart). However, because the romance was cut from the final script, the scene is robbed of much of the power it might have held. As it stands, the pardon scene demonstrates only that Lincoln's passion to preserve the Union never overwhelmed his compassion for his fellow man. Another obvious means by which Griffith might have driven home the same point would have been Lincoln's signing of the Emancipation Proclamation and the subsequent freeing of the slaves. Griffith references both events, but in a tone that could hardly be less celebratory.

After the dramatic pardoning scene, Griffith offers just one scene of slaves, legs shackled together, singing a song about Moses leading the Israelites out of Egypt. Because this scene, which seems to the modern viewer very benign, was deemed controversial because of its depiction of the conditions of slavery, it was removed from the film for many of its initial showings, and it remains missing from many surviving film and video copies. It is followed by a scene in which a somber Lincoln reads aloud from the Emancipation Proclamation, signs it, and then utters, "Well, gentlemen, it is done." That is the totality of Griffith's presentation of Lincoln as the Great Emancipator. One can almost imagine Griffith delivering the same line to his crew after the scene was shot.

Lincoln next provides an unusual scene with General Ulysses S. Grant in which Lincoln's image as Savior of the Union is articulated most interestingly. Lincoln promotes Grant to lieutenant general—making him the first to hold that rank since George Washington, which indirectly associates Lincoln with the Founding Fathers—and appoints him leader of the suffering Union army. When Lincoln looks to the heavens and utters, "Thy will be done," Grant looks directly at Lincoln and responds, "*Thy* will be done." Like many Lincoln films, Griffith's talkie goes to great lengths to demonstrate Lincoln's faith. Indeed, religious rhetoric emerges often in the dialogue, especially during the war sequence. Yet Grant's response to Lincoln may be the most explicit comparison between Lincoln and a higher being found in any of the major Lincoln films.

Grant's assault, combined with the successful efforts of General Philip Sheridan is too powerful for the Confederate army. General Robert E. Lee soon accepts defeat and, in an act of mercy reminiscent of Lincoln's pardon, he orders that no more Union soldiers or spies be killed. Just as the historical Lincoln never publicly assigned blame to the South for the Civil War, fellow Kentuckian Griffith is equally generous in his articulation of the role the South played during and after the war. The Civil War sequence concludes with a scene at the White House in which Lincoln tells Grant that he looks forward to "welcoming back" the South as if it had never been gone. When Grant suggests that they make an example of Jefferson Davis and his generals, the president tells him, "Someone will have to shoot Abraham Lincoln first." After that obvious foreshadowing, audiences know that the film has but one final event to cover.

Ford's Theatre

The assassination sequence begins where one might expect: with an enraged Southern actor thirsty for revenge. Huddled in a cramped room somewhere in Virginia, John Wilkes Booth tells a small band of conspirators, "The man who kills Abraham Lincoln will be an immortal." Meanwhile, Lincoln is dining with his family in the White House; wife Mary Todd scolds, "Now, Mr. Lincoln, don't you go thinking about those dreams again. You'll live to be a hundred."

For whatever reason, screenwriters seem unable to avoid drawing comparisons between Lincoln's assassination and the killing of Julius Caesar. In *Abe Lincoln in Illinois* Stephen A. Douglas likens Lincoln to Brutus during their senatorial debates. But in *Abraham Lincoln* it is Booth who compares his plot to kill Lincoln with the death of Caesar. Booth tells his companions, "Tonight will be remembered throughout the ages. I play my best part. How much better a dagger would look. Cassius used a dagger, but this [Booth's revolver] is safer."

The inevitable assassination scene opens with the film's third and final on-screen date: "April 14, 1865." After taking his place in a balcony at Ford's Theatre, Lincoln stands and addresses the cheering crowd. His speech is a patchwork of familiar phrases from his second inaugural address and the Gettysburg Address. The only explanation for this clumsy recontextualization comes in the speech's humorously awkward introduction: "Again I—I say, with malice toward none, with charity for all, with firmness in the right as God gives us to see the right, we shall bind up the nation's wounds and cherish peace. That government of the people, by the people, and for the people shall not perish from the earth. Thank you. God bless you all." Why Griffith and Benét chose to represent Lincoln's final public moment as a collection of memorable sound bites, a "greatest hits" drawn from moments in history, is not known. But this is how Griffith's Lincoln bid farewell to the fictional audience in Ford's Theatre and, by extension, the very real audiences that first watched *Abraham Lincoln* in movie theaters.

The remainder of the film unfolds as expected. Booth enters the theater unnoticed and makes his way toward the president's box. He produces a revolver, shoots Lincoln, leaps to the stage, and shouts, "Sic semper tyrannis!" before fleeing.

The film's penultimate scene takes us back to where our story began: a humble cabin in Kentucky, this time to depict Lincoln's symbolic rebirth. The final scene begins with a dissolve from Lincoln's simple cabin to his imposing memorial in Washington, D.C. Music that moves from somber to celebratory announces the savior's resurrection.

Lincoln's legendary address at Gettysburg was initially judged a failure. According to Waldo W. Braden, "We must concede that many of the fifteen thousand people present on November 19, 1863, expressed little reaction to what Lincoln said in less than three minutes." Time, however, has given Lincoln's masterpiece its due. "Its power," Braden concludes, "is in its simple thought, composition, and language." "The sober, meditative Lincoln both by mood and word expressed contriteness, selflessness, and good taste—without oratorical flourish or pomposity. This reserve was his way of giving full respect to the 'honored dead' and to the ideal of freedom."[35]

Griffith's film has suffered the opposite fate. It received high praise from critics in 1930, but audiences did not flock to theaters as they had to see *The Birth of a Nation* fifteen years earlier. Now, as the film drifts steadily further into our collective past, its style is regarded as quaint and its narrative as dull. No doubt the inclusion of more bullets, blood, and bodies would have added to the spectacle of the war and perhaps to the legacy of the film, but instead of another sweeping war epic Griffith delivered a careful character study.

The film's critics maintain that Griffith's "utter reverence for his subject makes Lincoln appear somewhat stilted, as if posing dramatically for individual scenes, for posterity, to satisfy the image embedded in the public mind."[36] I do not deny that Griffith's Lincoln is somewhat stilted, nor that he has been posed dramatically as if for posterity. However, I do not concede that Griffith's Lincoln satisfies an image already embedded in the public mind. Rather, *Abraham Lincoln* seems to have lobbied its audience to choose its preferred vision, to embrace just one of the many images of Lincoln that were competing for the central place in the popular assessment.

By accident or design, Griffith greatly obscured Lincoln's role as the Great Emancipator. The experiences suffered by the film's young Lincoln had everything to do with the pain of personal loss and little to do with the injustice of political inequality. The Civil War fought in this film is not a battle over slavery but rather a conflict to hold the Union together. Even the brief and unusual final "speech" delivered by Lincoln all but guaranteed that audiences of the film would leave the theater just as visitors to the nation's capital would leave the newly erected Lincoln Memorial: remembering how Lincoln preserved the Union, and very likely giving little thought, if any, to how he freed the slaves.

We know beyond doubt that the memorial was intentionally designed to accomplish this interpretive mission. We do not know if it was Griffith's intention to echo the memorial's memory work, but it does so regardless. Together, the Lincoln Memorial (completed in 1922) and *Abraham Lincoln* (released in 1930) encouraged an entire generation of Lincoln lovers to remember unity and not freedom as the greatest gift he had bequeathed to them.

4

Great Commoner

Young Mr. Lincoln (1939)

> It was, said an observer, as if two mental tickets were issued for Lincoln, one giving access to the almost superhuman savior of the Union and sad-eyed emancipator, the other to the droll humorist and the "great heart" who subsumed reason to sentiment. "Some of our countrymen pin their faith to one ticket, some to the other, and some—such is the delightful inconsistency of the human mind—accept both."
>
> —Merrill D. Peterson, *Lincoln in American Memory*

Lincoln's story always was one of a tall man and a long shadow, but recently Lincoln scholars have been inspecting the shadow as meticulously as the man. Indeed, Lincoln's image—or images—in our collective memory has become increasingly interesting to Lincoln scholars from varied disciplines. That image in American collective memory has evolved constantly over the past century and a half, and the consequences for both the man and the nation he has come to represent can hardly be overestimated. Although his image has known many manifestations, perhaps the most complicated is his representation as simultaneously ordinary and extraordinary: the Great Commoner.[1]

This chapter examines John Ford's 1939 film *Young Mr. Lincoln* to analyze how the film encourages its audience to make sense of the Lincoln it creates. *Young Mr. Lincoln* fashions the quintessential image of Lincoln as the Great Commoner, an image that will be explored in great detail in this chapter. Ford's film work falls well within the classical Hollywood tradition; he became a master of its invisible style, using cinematic techniques and narrative structures that were familiar to audiences well trained in the collaborative process through which moving images acquire textual and cultural meaning. Even a viewer entirely unacquainted with Lincoln—if such a viewer could possibly have existed in 1939—could easily have made sense of Ford's representation of Lincoln provided that viewer possessed even a rudimentary understanding of the classical style.

Still, the question of how we are to make sense of a Lincoln who is presented as seamlessly and simultaneously great and common is a far more complex matter. Indeed, the popular image of Lincoln as the Great Commoner is fraught with contradictions, and few artists have managed to reconcile them. How Ford manages to accomplish this has fascinated and perplexed critics of his film. In this chapter, I posit that a theory of dialectical cinema may begin to reveal the remarkable way in which Ford's film succeeds where others have failed.

The Logic of Lincoln

The great Soviet filmmaker Sergei Eisenstein believed that it is "art's task to make manifest the contradictions of Being. To form equitable views by stirring up contradictions within the spectator's mind, and to forge accurate intellectual concepts from the dynamic clash of opposing passions."[2] More than any other Hollywood film about Abraham Lincoln, *Young Mr. Lincoln* explores—and seems to try to explain—the complicated image of the Great Commoner. Even the film's title hints that audiences will encounter a Lincoln divided. Ford's character is met in both adolescence and adulthood: the boy is at once naive and already in possession of the wit and wisdom for which the man is remembered.

However, dual conceptions of Lincoln are not unusual. He is often remembered and portrayed as both "apart [from] and a part of the people."[3] Even Karl Marx, whose writings on Hegel helped inspire Eisenstein's interest in the dialectic, described Lincoln as "one of the rare men who succeed in becoming great, without ceasing to be good."[4] Despite the popularity of this incarnation, a seamless blend of the ordinary and the extraordinary is not easily managed in life or art. "Common, weak men cannot represent great and powerful nations; elitist strongmen cannot represent democracies. Lincoln's image was for these reasons pulled in contrary directions: toward stateliness, authority, and dignity on the one hand, and toward plainness, familiarity, and homeliness on the other. This dualism showed up in countless biographies and articles about Lincoln's life, but it was revealed more vividly by pictorial devices."[5] It is precisely at the crossroads of these two different Lincolns that Ford located his film. How he negotiated the apparent contradiction in his subject is central to Ford's treatment of Lincoln. This chapter contends that the film produces not only the mere depiction of Lincoln's dualism but, more important, the demonstration of multiple methods for resolving the "delightful inconsistency" thought to be inherent in Lincoln's image as both great and common.[6]

Mimetic syntax in literary studies involves the imitation of textual content by textual form. In literature, a mimetic text is one in which "sentence structure reinforces either the state of a character's mind, or the actions which a character is undertaking."[7] Visual media operate differently. David Bordwell organizes basic theories of film narration in this way: "*Diegetic* theories conceive of narration as consisting either literally or analogically of verbal activity: a telling. . . . *Mimetic* theories conceive of narration as the presentation of a spectacle: a showing. Note, incidentally, that since the difference applies only to 'mode' of imitation, either theory may be applied to any medium."[8] In *Young Mr. Lincoln,* the film's narrative content and structure mimic the historical Lincoln's alleged state of being. Ford achieves this through the clever and repeated use of what Eisenstein described when writing about dialectical montage.

Dialectical Montage

The logic of Hegel's dialectic, which the Soviet filmmaker first encountered in the writings of Karl Marx, was relatively simple. Eisenstein himself described it in this way: "The dialectic is a way of looking at human history and experience as a perpetual conflict in which a force (thesis) collides with a counterforce (antithesis) to produce from their collision a wholly new phenomenon (synthesis) that is not the sum of two forces, but something greater than and different from them both."[9] But if the logic of the dialectic was simple, its application to images in general and narrative cinema in particular was anything but. After all, how could film, which relies on the visual reproduction of things concrete, possibly produce synthesized abstractions?

It was Eisenstein's contention that dialectical montage could liberate film—and might one day do the same for the societies that produced and consumed films—through the juxtaposition of radically disparate images. As Eisenstein saw it, if the combination of the words *child* (concrete) and *mouth* (concrete) produce *scream* (abstract) in the Chinese language, so too could the use of dialectical montage juxtapose two concrete objects so as to induce in the mind of the viewer a third abstract concept (for example, peace or freedom). Thus, by encouraging viewers to focus their gaze upon that which could not be seen, Eisenstein's theory of montage promised to enlarge the cinema's communicative potential by greatly expanding its vocabulary. In the process, it would transform mere movies into potent sites for serious social and political commentary.

Although ambitious, Eisenstein's efforts ultimately failed, at least from his own perspective. Few film historians deny him his rightful place among the most accomplished and influential filmmakers in the history of the medium. Although Eisenstein directed only seven feature films, including *Battleship Potemkin, October, Ivan the Terrible, Part I,* and *Ivan the Terrible, Part II,* his work forever changed the way movies were made and watched. Still, if Eisenstein's goal was to inspire a cultural and political uprising of Marxist proportions, such a revolution did not occur. Eisenstein himself eventually conceded that his work never fully realized the cinema's rhetorical potential. As he saw it, his defeat came not because dialectical montage was an insufficient weapon but rather because he had waged his war on the wrong battlefield: "All the available evidence indicates that the technique . . . will work only when it is firmly grounded in some specific narrative or dramatic context."[10]

Where was this dramatic context to be constructed if not in the Soviet state-sanctioned film industry? It was of course already under production in the dream factories of the Hollywood studio system. Eisenstein believed that whole films, as well as autonomous sequences within them, could be constructed according to his theory of the dialectic.[11] The classical Hollywood style that had come to define the American studio film would provide the means to achieve this end. And of all the great filmmakers to work within that system and according to that style, none realized Eisenstein's dream with more artistic beauty and rhetorical force than John Ford.

Ford's *Young Mr. Lincoln* brought the concept of dialectical montage—which he had encountered in the films and possibly the writings of Eisenstein—to bear upon his more conventional narrative style of filmmaking. Ford demonstrated that the dialectic enabled Lincoln, whose image as the Great Commoner was plagued by possible contradictions, to appear to the viewer as natural and harmonious. Ford thus succeeded in producing on film what Eisenstein only theorized: Lincoln's innate commonness (thesis), juxtaposed with his emerging greatness (antithesis), could produce a Lincoln different from and greater than the sum of his parts: the Great Commoner (synthesis).

Beyond Criticism

Young Mr. Lincoln may have shaped twentieth-century America's sense of Lincoln as significantly as the writings of Sandburg, doing so in ways that remain less obvious and therefore more consequential. Despite its title, the film is not a straightforward biopic. In fact, it places a fictional trial, not the factual Lincoln, at the center of its narrative. The story unfolds as follows: Abe Lincoln is a young lawyer of little experience when he agrees to defend two brothers accused of the same murder. Although the circumstances of the crime make it apparent that only one of the boys can be guilty, neither of them will speak to their lawyer or to the authorities. The fate of both thus hinges on Lincoln's instincts and on the pivotal testimony of two eyewitnesses to the crime—one of whom is the boys' own mother.

D. W. Griffith's biopic about Lincoln concentrates on familiar events of the president's adult life. Griffith later admitted that films like his produce little or no suspense because the "audience already knows what is going to happen."[12] But the same is not true of Lincoln's early life, about which very little is known. Thus, Ford's film is able to furnish suspense in part because it is about Lincoln's early years but also because it is not factual. Even audiences well versed in Lincoln lore are able to watch with anticipation as the Lincoln they know so well struggles to win a trial that never was.

Despite *Time* magazine's prediction that the "world should little note, nor long remember the story of *Young Mr. Lincoln,*" the film has come to be regarded as an American classic whose place in history is due in part to the political and ideological context in which it was conceived and received.[13] "Federal centralism, isolationism, economic reorganisation (including Hollywood), strengthening of the Democrat-Republican opposition, new threats of internal and international crisis, crisis and restrictions in Hollywood itself; such was the fairly gloomy context of the *Young Mr. Lincoln* undertaking."[14] Further complicating matters, Ford's film opened on the heels of a successful Broadway play about Lincoln penned by the outspoken Democrat Robert E. Sherwood. One theory holds that 20th Century-Fox, led by conservative producer Darryl F. Zanuck, tried to counter the effect of Sherwood's liberal play and to participate "in the Republican offensive" by releasing a film in which Lincoln espoused political ideals that complemented the 1940 Republican Party platform.[15]

Young Mr. Lincoln has proven to be fascinating to academics. Biographers of the film's director and leading actor rarely fail to point to it as evidence of their artistry.[16] Political historians continue to debate the film's possible influence on the 1940 presidential election as well as the accuracy and quality of its representation of Lincoln.[17] More intriguing is the emergence of a meta-critical subgenre that consists entirely of essays that critique critiques of the film. Indeed, the attention that scholars across the spectrum have given to Ford's film is exceeded only by the attention they have given to one another.[18]

However, the lively debate nearly ended in 1970 when the editors of the French film journal *Cahiers du cinéma* collectively authored an analysis of *Young Mr. Lincoln* that was so influential it all but ended academic discussion of the film's content and context. That famous essay—"John Ford's *Young Mr. Lincoln:* A Collective Text by the Editors of *Cahiers du Cinéma*"—examines the social and political climate in the United States in 1939 and offers a meticulous reading of the narrative. To this day, the essay "is recognized as one of the sites where philosophical, literary, political and psychoanalytic discourses that defined French intellectual culture in the late 1960s converged."[19]

In the essay's wake, other critics attracted to *Young Mr. Lincoln* gravitated toward one of two extremes: most opted for meta-critical analyses that took issue with the Marxist/structuralist method employed in the *Cahiers* essay, while others limited their discussions of the film to the few minuscule aspects not directly confronted by the *Cahiers* editors.[20] These ranged from the function of musical links between scenes to the alleged construction of Lincoln's/Henry Fonda's body as an on-screen phallic symbol.[21] As scholars became committed either to challenging the French critical giant or to fighting for the scraps it left behind, *Young Mr. Lincoln* was almost abandoned in favor of the essay thought to have consumed it.

Young Mr. Lincoln remains important for a number of reasons, beginning with its enduring popularity. That it might have been part of an effort by the entertainment industry to alter the outcome of a presidential election gives it even greater cultural currency. But for those interested in popular movies and public memory, the story of *Young Mr. Lincoln* is important because it was written by mixing histories in a way that has not been seen before or since in a Lincoln film. The details of the trial around which the narrative centers were the result of the imaginative weaving of two separate incidents, as screenwriter Lamar Trotti found inspiration for the courtroom drama in Lincoln's early career and in his own.

As a young lawyer, Lincoln is believed to have argued and won a court case in which he used an almanac to discredit a witness testifying that he observed a murder on what was shown by Lincoln to be a moonless night.[22] But it was a young Trotti who had covered a murder trial in Georgia that resulted in the execution of two brothers because the sole witness, their mother, refused to testify and name the guilty party. The marriage of these two cases produced the case found in *Young Mr. Lincoln.*

Film scholar David Bordwell acknowledges that the film's rhetoric centers on its dilemmas, but finds that it "secretes certain incompatibilities" and ultimately "succumbs to ambivalence." He further laments: "Lincoln both incarnates the Law, and rises above it; he acts as a mother's son but also must stand in for a missing father. As the film works itself out in action and imagery, Lincoln becomes constituted by absences. There are significant omissions: his mother, his fabled origins, his stand on slavery, the outcome of his choices (between plaintiffs, pies, and brothers)."[23]

Nick Browne agrees that matters of choice are central to the film's rhetoric, but he finds fault with any approach that, like Bordwell's, depends upon reading the film's absences. "[A] logic that relates the said to the not said (in Althusser, the relation visible/invisible) is interpolated into the mechanism of textual determination. The adoption of this kind of critical apparatus effects a shift to a perspective not dictated by the terms that the film explicitly formulates."[24] Browne interprets the film in this way: "The place of the spectator is formulated through a similar (implied) theory of democratic representation: Lincoln and Ford as 'with' but 'above' 'the people,' speaking in a sense they hardly understand, for them."[25] Browne is correct that *Young Mr. Lincoln*'s rhetorical activity involves the construction of Lincoln as the Great Commoner—with but above the people. However, this analysis finds that Lincoln's construction rests not simply on the character's representation as both great and common but also on the character's responses to the numerous dilemmas that demonstrate for viewers how they might handle the quandary they find in their own understanding of Lincoln.

Edwin Black explains both the logic and consequences of reading a text from such a perspective. "The oppositional tensions that ferment within a universe of discourse are signaled by its vocabulary, especially its antonyms. Public/private, liberal/conservative, radical/moderate, individual/societal: such pairs of antonyms are the matrices of rhetorical activity. They signify fields of judgment. . . . They are symptoms of the capacity of language to support both an affirmation and a denial—a contradiction, either moiety of which is a linguistic possibility."[26]

Without question, it is the wonderfully complex play among the film's dichotomies and dilemmas that makes *Young Mr. Lincoln* a remarkable text. In the minds of a people willing to embrace the contradictory images that Lincoln has come to assume, the Great Commoner is, at least here, no longer a Lincoln divided. Eisenstein's theory had finally been put into practice, as the master of montage himself conceded: "Of all the American films made up to now this *Young Mr. Lincoln* is the film that I wish, most of all, to have made. . . . It immediately enthralled me with the perfection of its harmony and the rare skill with which it employed all the expressive means at its disposal. *And most of all for the solution of Lincoln's image.*"[27]

Great Commoner

The film's opening credits are followed by Rosemary and Stephen Vincent Benét's poem:

> If Nancy Hanks
> Came back as a ghost,
> Seeking news
> Of what she loved most,
> She'd ask first
> "Where's my son?
> What's happened to Abe?
> What's he done?" . . .
>
> "You wouldn't know
> About my son?
> Did he grow tall?
> Did he have fun?
> Did he learn to read?
> Did he get to town?
> Do you know his name?
> Did he get on?"

Aesthetically, the words are designed to appear as if etched onto a stone surface, upon which one sees the shadows of branches and leaves—already viewers are provided with the symbols of things both living and legendary. The music reinforces the dual theme: the credits are accompanied by a chorus singing "The Battle Cry of Freedom," which leaves little doubt as to the grandeur of the subject, but the poem is backed by an original score that by comparison is simple and sentimental.[28] The poem's content is also relevant in that it exemplifies one of two strategic rhetorical devices that are established almost immediately: the female perspective and the reaction shot.

The first device, the use of an explicitly female perspective, is introduced in the poem. One critic has argued that the "entire film unfolds as an answer to the fictional questions put by the dead mother [Nancy Hanks] and acted out in the present of the film."[29] Although Hanks plays no role in the narrative, her female (and maternal) perspective is taken up by the character of Abigail Clay, a motherly figure whom Lincoln will compare to Hanks. In addition, Lincoln's love interests (Ann Rutledge and Mary Todd) will serve to provide the audience with pivotal information about Lincoln that is not shown on the screen. The perspectives offered by these women, another critic argues, result in the creation of "a model spectator" that guides "the spectatorial project of reconciling the two contradictory images of Lincoln that are familiar to us all: 'plain Abe' . . . vs. 'the Great Emancipator.'"[30]

But the film's project of reconciliation is not as seamless as some critics may think, nor can it be attributed solely to the female perspective. Consider the *Cahiers* editors' explanation of the way the poem prepares the audience to encounter the question of Lincoln's duality. According to that analysis, the poem encourages the audience to choose between his two images. "The enumeration of questions . . . programmes the development of the film by designating Lincoln's problematic as being that of a choice: the interrogative form of the poem, like a matrix, generates a binary system (the necessity to choose between two careers, two pies, two plaintiffs, two defendants, etc.) according to which the fiction is organized."[31] What the *Cahiers* analysis here fails to acknowledge is that Lincoln subverts the supposed necessity to choose—through avoidance, synthesis, and transcendence—in nearly every binary set. Similarly, viewers are encouraged to resolve their competing conceptions of Lincoln by *not* choosing between them.

The second rhetorical device, the reaction shot, is used almost as soon as the narrative gets under way. In the film's first scene, a young and visibly nervous Lincoln is introduced by his law partner, John Stuart, and makes what seems to be his first political speech. His remarks are "meant not only for the spectators in the film, who are anyway absent from the screen, but also to involve the spectator of the movie, brought into the cinematic space" through techniques of framing.[32] Lincoln begins this way: "I presume y'all know who I am. I'm plain Abraham Lincoln." By inviting a comparison with Stuart, the film teaches viewers much about Lincoln. "It is clear from the very beginning of the film, through the comparison between Stuart's flowery and overblown political speech and 'plain Abraham Lincoln's,' that the film's rhetoric distinguishes itself from, and acts as a commentary on, the rhetorical uses of language and gesture that make up a certain political/theatrical system within the fiction."[33]

However, the function of the reaction shot is of even greater significance in this scene. If anything, Lincoln delivers an unenthusiastic speech ("If elected, I shall be thankful—if not, it'll be all the same") that is nevertheless received enthusiastically by his listeners. Immediately following the speech, the viewer is shown a shot of two children whose approval is obvious. Their reaction cues the viewer's, as will the reactions of a number of other characters throughout the film, most notably Abigail Clay.

"The first reverse shot of the film, to the smiling children, anticipates the function that the reaction shot will generally assume: the burden of creating belief . . . [as] the spectator is induced to take up the narrator's point-of-view in the text."[34] In other words, the film allows certain characters (mostly women) who watch Lincoln within the film to teach viewers how to respond to him. It is this encouragement to "take up the narrator's point-of-view" that initiates the process of inducing the viewer to later employ the very same strategies now used by Lincoln and revealed to the viewer through this invisible narrator.

And the logic of those strategies of reconciliation is reinforced even by the film's score.

> While (1) [the "Mr. Lincoln" theme] sounds noble and is consistently invoked to suggest the heroic capacities of the main character, its close and persistent proximity with (2) [the "Lincoln's Humor" theme] supplies a kind of comic corrective by implying that the mythic-historical Lincoln is also part of a rough-and-tumble country society. This connection-juxtaposition is featured at the very beginning of *Young Mr. Lincoln,* when an extended treatment of (1) is

heard under dialogue as Lincoln delivers his political stump speech. The tone of this exercise gradually becomes less formal, because of a comic woodwind segue and a shot of two laughing children; and the more relaxed strains of (2) emerge as the hero learns that some people (the Clays) wish to trade at his store.[35]

Natural Law and Human Law

This "trade" comes just after Lincoln's speech and finds him obtaining a copy of Blackstone's *Commentaries,* which represents the film's first major thematic dichotomy: natural law and human law.[36] The tension between "humanly crafted positive laws and more transcendent natural law principles has been passed down to us throughout Western civilization, and human beings have agonized over the nature, scope, and functions of these different rights and duties since time immemorial."[37]

During the film's early scenes, Lincoln is shown almost exclusively in natural settings: walking in the forest, chopping wood, lying on his back in the grass. This theme is common in the few Lincoln films that address his early life; most take great pains to establish Lincoln as a self-made man sprung from the earth. What is curious about this section of *Young Mr. Lincoln,* however, is that Lincoln is shown either reading or carrying his newly acquired law text in nearly all of these outdoor scenes.

The dichotomy functions in this way: "Reading, though recognized as a gift through which men have access to civilization, might obscure or even block access to the unwritten text of nature."[38] For the largely uneducated Lincoln, his introduction to reading in general and the law in particular signifies the potential for change that might come at the cost of his connection to nature and to his natural instincts. This tension reappears at several moments throughout the film, but Lincoln eventually will bring the forces of natural law and human law into alignment, as only the Great Commoner can, when he refers to an almanac (natural law) in order to win a legal case (human law). Hence the film's first major dilemma is not resolved until the closing scene, but resolution is achieved through *synthesis,* not a choice between two supposedly opposing forces.

Fate and Free Will

The poem with which the film opens hints at the second major thematic dichotomy addressed in the narrative: fate and free will. "Rosemary Benét's poem prefaces a future-perfect from the outset. . . . Of course *we* know the answers, we tell ourselves, but Ford tricks us, answering every question not in terms of 1865 but of 1837. . . . From our point of view, 1837 is in context of 1865, of what *shall* be; yet the film asks that we grasp 1837's happenings from the mother's point of view, implying that for her 1837 is a truer response to her questions than what happened later, because that future belonged to history, while this present belonged to Abe."[39]

It is precisely the struggle between that which belongs to history and that which belongs to Abe that *Young Mr. Lincoln* begins to explore when it turns to Lincoln's historically suspect relationship with Ann Rutledge. From Rutledge's initial greeting ("Hello Mr. Lincoln . . . Abe"), Lincoln's dual roles are emphasized. The characters' mutual interest is obvious, but more significant is the subtle way in which their awkward courtship teaches the viewer about Lincoln. As they stroll along a riverbank, Lincoln's attempts at self-deprecation are met repeatedly with words of admiration. Through an extended exchange, viewers experience Lincoln's humility as they hear Rutledge's testimony of his intelligence, humor, reputation, and ambition. Much as the politicians of Lincoln's day allowed surrogates to campaign on their behalf, *Young Mr. Lincoln* assigns Rutledge the relatively easy yet requisite role of lobbying the audience on Lincoln's behalf.

Once the film has established that Lincoln and Rutledge are in love, the tone of the narrative changes dramatically. Lincoln enters the frame carrying an ax in one hand and flowers in the other—like the hands of his statue at the Lincoln Memorial, he here displays opposing symbols. Lincoln, kneeling at Rutledge's grave (the cause and exact timing of her death are not clear to the audience), he proposes to balance a stick on one end and let it fall to the ground, pledging to Rutledge that if it falls toward the burial marker he will go to Springfield and practice law, but if it falls toward him he will stay in New Salem. Thus the tension between free will and fate that was introduced by the poem assumes a more tangible form, as it often does in Hollywood's biographical films.

The genre is that "of the 'early life of the great man,' not conceived as an education for his later life, but as an anecdotal revelation of his pre-adaptation for the role he is later to play."[40] However, it is questionable whether *Young Mr. Lincoln* adheres to the genre's basic formula. At least one of John Ford's biographers believes that "the movie's ultimate concern is the dubious dialectic between free will and a deterministic cosmos—between Lincoln as autonomous man and Lincoln as agent of history." "Destiny, as we know, is drawing him; but he himself is only gradually becoming aware of it."[41] But another critic argues: "This is the crux of the Lincoln myth: he *knows,* he *is,* he does not *learn;* that which he does learn will do him little good. What he *knows* on intuition, however, will take him to his fate."[42] Such variance in interpretations is not the result of whimsical readings. Rather, each response is solicited by a text in which the forces of both fate and free will are shown to be at work.

As *Young Mr. Lincoln*'s viewers suspect will happen, the stick Lincoln balances falls toward Rutledge's grave and sends him to Springfield. But just as it seems that fate has intervened and that the film has made a choice in telling Lincoln's story, Ford complicates matters. Lincoln confesses to Rutledge that he *might* have tipped it her way "just a little." Like the tension between natural law and human law, this dichotomy can be traced throughout the remainder of the film, with neither side ever overwhelming the other. But unlike that other dichotomy, which the film reconciled by synthesis, fate and free will are managed by evasion, with necessary choices somehow avoided by the characters and the film (and, by extension, the viewers as well).

A Lincoln Divided

After Lincoln's move to Springfield and entry into law, the film temporarily sets aside its exploration of thematic dichotomies and sharpens its focus on the consequential manner in which the protagonist handles more concrete dilemmas. From an on-screen title viewers learn that it is now April 12, 1837. At the law office he shares with John Stuart, Lincoln is shown reclining lazily in a rocking chair as two clients argue. At first Lincoln attempts to convince "brother Woolrich" and "brother Hawthorne," as he calls them (perhaps foreshadowing his future case involving two biological brothers), that each owes the other a specific amount of money and that "by a strange coincidence" his fee rounds out the difference. With logic and poise Lincoln is able to propose a solution that will avoid violence—and another choice. However, both men reject the proposal; one humorously threatens, "I'll learn the law first!" Shifting strategies, Lincoln rises from his chair and, towering above the men, asks, "Gentlemen, d'ya ever hear about the time in the Black Hawk War when I butted two fellas heads together—and busted both of 'em?" Brothers Woolrich and Hawthorne experience an immediate change of heart. It seems there's more than a little of the country rail-splitter left in this city lawyer.

According to the *Cahiers* analysis, this scene is instrumental in teaching the audience about how choices must be managed. "The scene insists on Lincoln's supreme *cleverness,* in resolving any situation, the Law being able to decide either by taking one side against the other, or like here, by craftily restoring the balance between the two sides of the scales. This second solution is obviously preferred by the film because it emphasises Lincoln's legendary unifying role."[43] The interpretation is partially correct: the film does prefer the second solution, restoring balance, but it does so in support of Lincoln's image not as the Great Emancipator (his legendary unifying role) but as the Great Commoner (a legendary role in need of unification).

The longest and most significant sequence in the film is made up of a series of short episodes that take place in a single day: Springfield's annual Independence Day parade and festival. It consists of five events: a parade, a pie-judging event, a rail-splitting contest, a tug-of-war, and tar-barrel burning. At the parade Lincoln greets several people, including a "Mr. Douglas." Although the famous Lincoln-Douglas debates of 1858 take place in a time after that dramatized in *Young Mr. Lincoln,* the two characters share a scene near the film's conclusion that foreshadows their eventual clash.

At the pie-judging event Lincoln appears on a stage that is decorated with banners, consistent with political rallies of the nineteenth century. The image is familiar and foretelling. But instead of an eloquent oration, Lincoln says, "At first I thought it was that apple [pie] for sure. And then

I sank my teeth into that peach and I just couldn't seem to make up my mind. So I sample the apple again." The man whose conviction regarding slavery was such that he was willing to accept civil war rather than compromise here seems incapable of choosing between pies. However, it quickly becomes evident that what plays like indecision is really a clever ploy to eat more than his fair share of pie—and to avoid yet another difficult choice.

During this contest the viewer is shown a brief but important scene that sets up the rest of the narrative. Two drunken men in the crowd bully the Clay family, the people who gave Lincoln the law book that changed his life. Although the commotion lasts several minutes, Lincoln takes no notice. But the episode proves significant later in the film.

At the rail-splitting contest Lincoln swings his ax less often and with less force than his opponents, but his blows are more methodical and precise. The symbolism of the log—divided in two equal parts—is not difficult to interpret. Nor is the outcome of the contest surprising; Lincoln defeats his opponents handily. The fourth event is a tug-of-war between the Hog Wallow Boys and the smaller and outnumbered Speed County Demons. It first appears that Lincoln will not be participating, but he soon takes up a position at the rear of the underdog Demons. In this rare case, Lincoln seems willing to choose between two sides, but in so doing he strikes a different kind of balance by playing dirty to ensure that the right side comes out the winner. After a long struggle, Lincoln secures his end of the rope to a wagon and sends the horse hitched to it on its way, propelling his opponents into the mud. Lincoln thus transcends the petty contest and scores a victory for all those who are smaller and outnumbered.

The film's producer, Darryl F. Zanuck, described the festival as "our only slow part of the picture," but Marsha Kinder argues that the games and contests "function as double symbolic substitutions for the battles he [Lincoln] will face both in the melodramatic context of the film's plot (the lynch scene and trial) and in the historic context of the Civil War (where he would become the Great Emancipator)."[44] The *Cahiers* editors state that the "principle of Justice (whether or not to choose) is realised [in this episode] through a series of derivatives which exhaust all its modalities."[45]

Repeatedly, Lincoln and the film have demonstrated for viewers that dichotomies and dilemmas rarely require a selection between the available options but instead can be resolved through strategies like avoidance, synthesis, or transcendence.

The festival's final event, tar-barrel burning, is of little significance and teaches the audience nothing about Lincoln. Instead, it "merely provides an atmospheric transition to the murder (a device suggested by Zanuck)."[46] However, it is during this event that the biography becomes a murder mystery. In a clearing in the woods, one of Abigail Clay's sons, Matt, wrestles with Scrub White, one of the drunken men who was shown harassing the Clays at the festival. The situation becomes dire when White produces a revolver. Sensing the likely result, Matt and his brother Adam tackle the armed man.

At this crucial moment the film forces the viewers' attention away from the fight, concealing it, and cuts to Abigail Clay's reaction—which viewers have been trained to use as a guide for their own response. We see her wince in horror at the sound of a gunshot. J. Palmer Cass, the other drunken troublemaker at the festival, arrives and announces, to the Clays' surprise, that Scrub White is dead—killed not by a gunshot but by a knife belonging to one of the Clay boys. As Cass screams bloody murder, the whole town comes to the scene of the crime.

Ford's treatment of the murder scene is fascinating. "[It] is literally *indescribable,* insofar as it is the realisation—through the succession and length of the shots, abrupt changes in angle, play on distance, the reactions, and the behaviour of the participants, the successive arrival of witnesses—of an amazing system of *deception* which affects all characters implicated in the event, and blinds them as well as the spectator. . . . Thus what is happening here is precisely the cinematic questioning of direct vision, of perception insofar as it conceals its structure."[47]

Although both characters and viewers believe they understand what has unfolded, all have been deceived. Viewers have been taught by the film to rely on the female perspective and the reaction shot for confirmation of their suspicions—a lesson Ford will reinforce in later scenes. But after the murder Ford offers a female reaction that is wrong, based on confusion, but initially the viewer does not realize that Abigail Clay is mistaken. The film does not exactly lie to viewers, but it does deliberately and cleverly mislead them.

Speech and Action

The film's final thematic dichotomy, speech and action, is introduced once Lincoln volunteers to represent the Clays at trial. But just minutes after the murder, an angry mob arrives at the jail prepared for a lynching. With wit, self-deprecating humor, and a threat of violence, Lincoln quells the crowd and cleverly persuades it to leave the boys to the judicial system.

The relationship between speech and action figures curiously within the dialogue. Blocking the mob's access to the jail door, Lincoln announces, "I'm not up here to make any speeches," but he proceeds to speak eloquently and effectively, dissuading the mob from following through on its murderous plan. When confronted by Big Buck, the strongest man in Springfield, Lincoln again disparages the use of words: "I thought I'd find that big mouth of yours around here tellin' people what to do." Yet Lincoln himself makes use of a variety of persuasive rhetorical appeals, and none is more effective than when he singles out a member of the mob. "For instance, you take Jeremiah Carter yonder. There's not a finer, more decent God-fearing man in Springfield than Jeremiah Carter. And I wouldn't be surprised if when he goes home he takes down a certain book and looks into it. Maybe he'd just happen to hit on these words, 'Blessed are the merciful, for they shall obtain mercy.' That's all I've got to say, friends. Good night." With these words the mob disbands.[48]

The scene demonstrates that Lincoln is willing and able to employ both physical force and the force of his rhetoric in the pursuit of justice, a clear form of synthesis. But it is in the context of the speech/action dichotomy that the strategy of transcendence is most fully realized. Here Lincoln redefines the mob's sense of self by reconstituting them as individuals within the larger, more sacred context of God's divine plan for all human beings. Later, at the trial, Lincoln comes full circle, returning to the film's original dichotomy of human laws and natural laws, by arguing that Abigail Clay's right to remain silent to protect her sons transcends the court's right to compel her testimony.

Before the trial begins Lincoln is featured in two very different social contexts that reinforce his duality: first at a formal ball with Mary Todd, Stephen Douglas, and the rest of Springfield's upper class, and later at the Clays' humble cabin in the woods. In each setting Lincoln seems at once in and out of his natural element. At the ball Lincoln holds court with a group of older men, amusing them with his humor. But he is laughably awkward as he dances "in the worst way" with Mary Todd. At the Clays' cabin Lincoln is at ease, even remarking how much the Clays remind him of his own family. But he is also unlike them in many ways. This difference is best illustrated when he is called upon to read a letter that Adam has written to his illiterate mother.

Before leaving, Lincoln confronts Abigail Clay about what she saw the night of the murder. Although she refuses to speak, Lincoln believes that he already knows the truth. Earlier in their conversation, Lincoln lured her into admitting that Adam was good with an ax, while Matt "was always the puny one." Abigail, in her refusal to testify at the trial, is not the only one who opts for silence over speech.[49] Amazingly, the film would have its audience believe that during their stay in jail, although they occupied the same cell, the Clay brothers never discuss the murder. We are to assume that because each brother knows he is innocent, each supposes the other guilty. And of course the film itself is silent about the murder, removing it from our view and concealing the truth until the very end.

At trial Lincoln and the opposing attorney question potential jurors, the last of whom is a shabby-looking man who never speaks, only nodding his head in silence. The eloquent Lincoln accepts him immediately. After opening statements, witnesses begin to be questioned. Eventually the prosecution calls Abigail Clay and tries to force her to reveal which son is guilty. But Lincoln, whose eloquence saved her sons from the mob, defends her right to silence by describing her as a woman "who says little but does much." Browne argues that Lincoln is "inscribed in the trial as the voice of the inarticulate mother."[50] But Lincoln does not defend her sons because Abigail Clay cannot. Rather, Lincoln argues that her right to silence trumps the court's right to force her testimony. It is therefore not a matter of guilt or innocence that Lincoln addresses—it is rather a fundamental issue of right and wrong that he places before the jury—one element of a larger question that was first raised as he read Blackstone's *Commentaries* and remarked, "Gee whiz, that's all there is to it, rights and wrongs."

On the final day of the trail Lincoln calls J. Palmer Cass to the stand for a third time and accuses him, to the surprise of everyone in the courtroom, of murdering his friend Scrub White. Earlier Cass had testified that he had been able to witness the murder because the evening sky was "moon bright." Returning to the initial dichotomy of human laws and natural laws, Lincoln produces a copy of the *Farmer's Almanac,* the antithesis of Blackstone's *Commentaries,* which states that on the night of the murder the moon was only in its first quarter and had set before the killing occurred. Cornered, Cass admits his guilt and the Clay boys are set free. The narrative ends as Lincoln walks up a hill into a symbolic raging storm. A chorus sings "The Battle Hymn of the Republic" as we are treated to an image of the Lincoln Memorial, foreshadowing what awaits both the man and his nation.

Great and Common

It is clear that Lincoln's duality, as it is depicted in Ford's film, involves the juxtaposition of an innate commonness with an emerging greatness. That the film presents Lincoln in this way—not one thing, nor the other, but both—is not surprising. Hollywood has a long history of trying to have it both ways. However, what is unusual is the manner in which this film assists the viewer first in recognizing the dialectical nature of the character and then, more remarkably, how it rehearses with the viewer multiple methods of resolving the dialectic, including avoidance, synthesis, and transcendence. The film, in what might be Lincoln's most complicated incarnation, engages its audience in a dual act of instruction: demonstrating first that Lincoln is possessed of a dual nature, and second that multiple means are available to resolve the potential incompatibility.

Which pie does Lincoln choose? Neither. Which career, law or politics, does he choose? Both. Which brother is guilty of murder? Lincoln will not even entertain the discussion, challenging instead the very grounds upon which the truth of the matter is being sought. In all of these cases and many more, the film displays for its viewers several means available to them for resolving the film's central dichotomy: Lincoln, the Great Commoner. Thus, as Abe solves the mystery in *Young Mr. Lincoln* (the murder), viewers are prepared to solve the mystery of young Mr. Lincoln (his duality). Ford's Lincoln may be troubling historically, but he logically reflects a singularly complex image that has come to define the man in American public memory.

It is fitting that the film concludes with the image of the Lincoln Memorial—more fitting, perhaps, than Ford may have realized. Although the structure, with its towering statue of the president, generally is understood to immortalize Lincoln, it was in fact erected with a simpler message in mind: unification. *Young Mr. Lincoln* appropriately culminates with an image that emphasizes harmony: a combination of different elements forming a perfect whole. Understood within this context, the film's conclusion is a final punctuation to its central theme regarding the logic of Lincoln's image and essence as both great and common.

Young Mr. Lincoln remains a remarkable work of popular art and public memory. Although Lincoln scholars typically slight the effect that it and other films have had in shaping Lincoln's image (if they address such texts at all), Ford's film represents the rhetorical possibilities embodied in popular forms. If we neglect such texts, we willingly sacrifice an understanding of how our collective memory of Lincoln continues to be shaped by the cinema.

5

First American

Abe Lincoln in Illinois (1940)

> Having seen Sherwood's play [*Abe Lincoln in Illinois*], and having noticed how the audience itself participated, I believe it carries some shine of the American dream, that it delivers great themes of human wit, behavior and freedom, with Lincoln as mouthpiece and instrument.
>
> —Carl Sandburg, foreword to *Abe Lincoln in Illinois,* by Robert E. Sherwood

Abe Lincoln in Illinois (1940) depicts Lincoln's formative years—his prairie years. The film adaptation of Robert E. Sherwood's Pulitzer Prize-winning play, the movie takes on an overwhelming task: representing a life as it grew into a legend. As the film begins, Lincoln is an unsophisticated young man of little experience. As it ends, the president-elect is departing by rail for the White House. Covering the transformative years in between, the film presents a Lincoln who is as mythical as he is historical. Although very much a selective reworking of recorded history, *Abe Lincoln in Illinois* still ranks among the more accurate of all of the Hollywood films that examine Lincoln's early life. Merrill D. Peterson, historian and author of *Lincoln in American Memory,* argues that when compared to the more popular *Young Mr. Lincoln* (1939), *Abe Lincoln in Illinois* "takes itself seriously, and is a better historical drama."[1]

In the supplementary notes that accompany the published version of his script written for the stage, Sherwood acknowledges that he is not a "learned biographer" and that the play freely takes advantage of dramatic license.[2] However, he also outlines the historical sources he consulted while writing his play, and his notes on the origins of the speeches delivered by Lincoln and Stephen A. Douglas in this work are particularly interesting. John Cromwell's film departs rather substantially from its theatrical forebear, but nevertheless the overall structure of play and film is the same. Carl Sandburg understood precisely what made them both work: "how the audience itself participated."

Abe Lincoln in Illinois is a fascinating film, in part because it is largely incoherent unless its audience is familiar with the major details of Abraham Lincoln's life (and death) in Washington, D.C.—a period not covered in the film. Cromwell's film thus violates one of the fundamental rules governing the classical Hollywood cinema: it insists that its audience understand much of its action (the events of Lincoln's life in Illinois) within the context of its absences (the events of Lincoln's life in Washington, D.C.). Like promises unfulfilled, the events of Lincoln's future are referenced repeatedly, but they are never depicted on the screen.

Those able to provide the missing pieces of the puzzle are called upon to engage in a most complicated kind of memory work, recalling simultaneously what occurred *earlier* in the film and *later* in history. Of course, most American filmgoers in 1940 would have had little trouble completing the picture. Still, even if the audience was up to the challenge Cromwell placed before it, this is a film that asked much more of the viewer than did the typical Hollywood narrative of that era. Indeed, *Abe Lincoln in Illinois* demands that its audience possess an unusual ability: it must be able to remember the future.

Furthermore, the film presents the figure of Lincoln in a manner very similar to the narrative itself: as transcending time. Specifically, Lincoln is constructed in the image of the First American: not only the direct ideological descendent of the Founding Fathers but also the physical embodiment of the political ideals they created in the Revolutionary era. Both story and character, in other words, exist in the present while resonating with the American past and future.

The Rugged Path

For many Americans living in the mid-twentieth century, Raymond Massey *was* Abraham Lincoln. What few know now is that he almost wasn't. Delighted to have been offered the coveted Broadway role by Sherwood, with whom he had already collaborated in *Idiot's Delight,* Massey accepted with much enthusiasm. However, when the *Daily Times* discovered that Massey had been cast as the representative American, its editorial title asked, "A Canadian as Abraham Lincoln?" Massey later wrote: "The editorial allowed I was a fine actor and looked like Lincoln; but suggested that as a Canadian, little better than an Englishman, I would soon run into prejudice. Under the actor's photograph was the caption, 'Good—but not Lincoln.'"[3]

Sherwood's play borrowed heavily from Carl Sandburg's *Abraham Lincoln: The Prairie Years,* and was almost called "The Rugged Path." The phrase is from John Keats's poem "On Death," one of Sherwood's favorites. But it was *Abe Lincoln in Illinois* that opened on October 15, 1938, at the Plymouth Theatre in New York City. The production would go on to become a critical and commercial success, enjoying no fewer than 472 performances.

Massey nearly missed them all. He had taken his preparations for the difficult role very seriously. He later wrote: "I tried to keep my Lincoln simple. I had done no research beyond reading Carl Sandburg's *The Prairie Years* and the Lincoln books that everyone reads. I relied on Bob [Sherwood] to supply the character in his script. I have always feared over-embellishment of a character, having seen some brilliant performances of historical characters marred by excess of detail and self-conscious emphasis."[4] Despite a standing ovation and repeated curtain calls after a dress rehearsal at the National Theatre in Washington, D.C., Massey asked to be replaced. His problems were psychological: it seems that even the towering Massey found Lincoln's figure a daunting one to embody. (A year later, Henry Fonda would experience a similar wave of panic while watching footage from the first day's shoot on *Young Mr. Lincoln.*) But eventually Sherwood and director Elmer Rice convinced Massey to remain with the production. Two weeks after the play's debut the actor even received something of a public apology from the *Daily News.* Said Massey, "It was a most thorough ingestion of crow and I heartily enjoyed it."[5]

Sherwood sold the rights to the film version of his story to RKO Radio for $250,000—a fortune in the late 1930s. After the deal was completed there remained the crucial question of who would portray Lincoln. Massey did not expect to be offered the role. "In trade papers and gossip columns, about the only star who was not mentioned as a probability for the screen Abe was W. C. Fields, in spite of his identification with a stovepipe hat."[6] In the end, and at Sherwood's insistence, Massey did indeed reprise the role for Hollywood and eventually went on to be nominated for an Academy Award. Massey was made ready for the screen with the help of Norman Rockwell, who produced a commissioned portrait that combined Lincoln's and Massey's most striking features. The iconic image served as a model for the film's makeup artists.

Although Sherwood had won the casting battle, the scripting war proved to be another matter. With the help of screenwriter Grover Jones, with whom Sherwood shared an equal writing credit, the play's twelve scenes were reshaped dramatically. Massey was not pleased with the changes. "I will never understand why a collaboration was needed in the writing of the screenplay of *Abe Lincoln in Illinois*. The resulting script was very good but somehow the inevitable expansion of the action, the splitting up of the tightly compact scenes of the stage play which the screen version was supposed to demand, seemed to accentuate rather than diminish the episodic nature of the play."[7] Massey was especially surprised and disappointed by one particular change: the omission of a crucial prayer scene: the only scene in the play, in fact, that had been born entirely of the playwright's imagination.

Sherwood, believing that the missing year between the initial date set for Lincoln's wedding and the date he actually wed Mary Todd offered an opportunity for dramatic invention, used that opportunity to invent "the pivotal scene in his play" in which an irresolute Lincoln was shown praying for the life of a sick boy and, in the process, for the future of the country.[8] Lincoln's prayer was delivered on the stage as follows:

> Oh, God, the father of all living, I ask you to look with gentle mercy upon this little boy who is here, lying sick in this covered wagon. His people are travelling far, to seek a new home in the wilderness, to do your work, God, to make this earth a good place for your children to live in. They can see clearly where they're going, and they're

> not afraid to face all the perils that lie along the way. I humbly beg you not to take their child from them. Grant him the freedom of life. Do not condemn him to the imprisonment of death. Do not deny him his birthright. Let him know the sight of great plains and high mountains, of green valleys and wide rivers. For this little boy is an American, and these things belong to him, and he to them. Spare him, that he too may strive for the ideal for which his fathers have labored, so faithfully and for so long. Spare him and give him his fathers' strength—give us all strength. Oh God, to do the work that is before us. I ask you this favor, in the name of *your* son, Jesus Christ, who died upon the Cross to set men free. Amen.[9]

As Massey saw it, the prayer functioned within the play as an answer to the question "How did this man of doubt and indecision, this shiftless fellow, become a man of passionate conviction?" The decision to remove the scene from the film was to Massey an "incredible blunder" that turned a complex story into "a procession of episodes."[10]

On January 21, 1940, one day before the film premiered in Washington, D.C., a special screening was held at the White House. Sherwood described the evening in his diary:

> *Jan. 21, 1940.* Washington—Dined tonight at the White House. Sat next to Mrs. Roosevelt, Madeline [Sherwood] next to the President. For dinner—scrambled eggs & sausages, cold meats, salad, lousy white wine (probably Californian). . . . Picture of *Abe* run off after dinner in hall on second floor. Mrs. R. said that some representatives of the Virginia hunting set had been brought there by Franklin D. Jr. to see *Gone With the Wind* and after they left she said to the President, "People like that make me feel like turning Communist," and he said "Me too." He (the President) said he'd like to have the text of the Debate speeches to read over the radio. All evidently like the picture enormously, & it deserves to be liked. John Cromwell there, too & he certainly deserves honors. I liked it much better the second time & a title has been inserted at my suggestion which helps a lot.[11]

Massey's recollection of the evening is slightly different. He later wrote: "Bob [Sherwood] and I sat next to President Roosevelt at the screening. He was in jovial spirits and seemed to enjoy the picture. He muttered, 'He wrote those speeches himself!' It was the second time I had seen the film and the loss of the prayer seemed more damaging than ever. I looked at Bob. His head was bowed, his eyes closed."[12]

The following day Massey escorted Eleanor Roosevelt to the film's premiere at Keith's Theatre in Washington, D.C. Outside the theater they were met by a sizable crowd of protestors. It was not the content of the film but rather the conditions under which it was to be viewed that brought forth the picketers. Because of the Jim Crow laws still in effect, African Americans were prohibited from sitting in the general audience. The life of the Great Emancipator was thus viewed from racially segregated seating.

Active Viewers

Whether one considers *Abe Lincoln in Illinois* merely a progression of episodes or something more complex depends on the critical perspective that is brought to the film. This chapter explores the structure of the work, examining the action within the film as well as the actions invited between the film and its audience. Such an analysis reveals a film more complex and interesting than a mere collection of historic moments.

Roland Barthes has argued that a collaborative perspective "utterly transforms the modern text." He explains the transformation as it occurs in relation to literature: "We know now that a text is not a line of words releasing a single 'theological' meaning (the 'message' of the Author-God) but a multidimensional space in which a variety of writings, none of them original, blend and clash. . . . Thus is revealed the total existence of writing: a text is made of multiple writings, drawn from many cultures and entering into mutual relations of dialogue, parody, contextation, but there is one place where this multiplicity is focused and that place is the reader, not, as was hitherto said, the author."[13] Barthes was not arguing for an unlimited range of meanings; of course, valid interpretations are those that can be justified textually and contextually. But the most interesting texts are usually sufficiently complex and ambiguous to allow for, if not invite, a range of possible interpretations.

Film scholar David Bordwell explains how the concept of the co-creation of meanings relates to the classical Hollywood cinema: "The Hollywood spectator, it is claimed, is little more than a receptacle; few skills of attention, memory, discrimination, inference-drawing, or hypothesis-testing are required. Now this is clearly too simple. Classical films call forth activities on the part of the spectator. These activities may be highly standardized and comparatively easy to learn, but we cannot assume that they are simple."[14] This is precisely what is meant by the action that occurs "between the film and its audience."

Recognizing that such action occurs leads to the realization that viewers are not limited to "reading [a film] to find a meaning or theme within the work as the solution to a sort of puzzle which has a right answer."[15] One of the most interesting consequences of the process of collaborative meaning making is that our conception of the narrative expands to become something more than the mere sum of its parts. "Narrative, taken in its broadest sense, must constantly work to produce a conventionalized economy between its two levels: the discourse, the material aspects of the telling, and the story, the product of this telling, the fiction told."[16]

Literary critics now known as the Russian formalists understood this when they distinguished between what they called a narrative's *fabula* and its *syuzhet,* or what I will here refer to as story and plot. Story (*fabula*) refers to "a pattern which perceivers of narratives create through assumptions and inferences. It is the developing result of picking up narrative cues, applying schemata, framing and testing hypotheses," while plot (*syuzhet*) designates the "actual arrangement and presentation of the fabula in the film . . . the organized set of cues prompting us to infer and assemble story information."[17]

It is the active viewer who responds to the content and style of a film's plot, and then co-creates the more complex story. All classical Hollywood films work in this way, but *Abe Lincoln in Illinois* is especially and uncommonly interesting in this regard. In addition to the usual work of story construction that all films demand of viewers, *Abe Lincoln in Illinois* requires that its viewers simultaneously filter the film through their knowledge of the historical Lincoln and the events of his life.

Abe Lincoln in Illinois's structure thus violates one of Hollywood's fundamental axioms: that narrative films must constitute a coherent whole, bringing resolution to most, if not all, of the major tensions established within them. This axiom is especially significant in the case of historical films, which often must provide viewers with a sufficient historical context within which its specific drama may be understood to unfold. As the historian Robert Rosenstone argues, one of the most significant features of "mainstream historical cinema" is that "Hollywood history is delivered in a story with a beginning, middle, and end. . . . The story is closed, completed, and ultimately, simple."[18]

Most classical films achieve an overall balance among the amount of information provided by their plot, the corresponding style of techniques, and the resulting story. What makes *Abe Lincoln in Illinois* unique among Lincoln films and rare among classical films is the dearth of information in its plot, which places an uncommon demand upon the viewer to co-create a meaningful story. In this sense, *Abe Lincoln in Illinois*'s plot functions as a first act that anticipates Lincoln's journey east, the secession of the South, the Civil War, the emancipation of the slaves, Lincoln's reelection, and his assassination. Unlike *Young Mr. Lincoln,* whose courtroom drama may be understood and enjoyed even by a viewer unfamiliar with Lincoln's political career because John Ford's film brought closure to the main story (the trial), *Abe Lincoln in Illinois* requires that audiences provide both the context and conclusion to its fragmented narrative.

Even when compared to the play upon which it is based, Cromwell's film creates a uniquely demanding relationship with its audience. One critic writing in 1940 observed that *Abe Lincoln in Illinois* "provides a number of subtleties" that in the stage version were "hurled . . . across the footlights."[19] Still, the play demanded a similar participation on the part of its audience. "Everyone who saw the play came into the theater with a sufficient store of knowledge regarding Lincoln to supply the information necessary for the unwritten fourth act, Lincoln's presidency, and fifth act,

Lincoln's death at the hands of an assassin. Audiences supplied the conclusion; and, indeed, because they were so fully aware of the conclusion . . . the irony of many of Lincoln's lines is greatly heightened and the dramatic tension is all-pervasive."[20]

In the film version, not only are Lincoln's lines "greatly heightened" with irony, many are meaningless unless the audience possesses that "store of knowledge" regarding his future.

First American

Sherwood's play consists of twelve scenes organized in three acts. Act 1 depicts Lincoln's personal life in New Salem, Illinois, during the 1830s; act 2 his personal life and legal career in Springfield, Illinois, during the 1840s; and act 3 his political experiences in Springfield between the years 1858 and 1861. Cromwell's film follows a similar structure. Like the play, it ends before Lincoln leaves for Washington. Also like the play, the film's fourth and fifth acts—Lincoln's presidency and assassination—are never played out but instead must be imagined by the audience even as it experiences the first three acts.

The narrative presents its hero as, above all, the First American. This conception of Lincoln is explained in *Lincoln in American Memory* in this way:

> The image of Lincoln as the First American proceeded from James Russell Lowell through Walt Whitman to Carl Sandburg. It belonged to the poets rather than to the preachers, historians, and politicians, though, of course, it radiated everywhere. Lowell had discerned the archetype of a new national character, one long imagined but only now realized in a man who looked at things, who related to people, who bore himself in ways indigenous to the American continent. The President who had spoken of "a new birth of freedom" was himself "new birth of our soil," and in that sense "the First American" authenticated the refounded nation. For it was only in the mirror of Lincoln, as Sandburg would say, that the American people finally came to see themselves.[21]

Act 1: New Salem

The film begins with production credits that appear over images in which humanity and nature are shown in harmonious coexistence. We see the silhouette of a man in a canoe crossing an otherwise still body of water; a deer sprinting through a grassy field; a covered wagon making its way over a hill and across a shallow stream; a small town. The frontier is being settled in these opening frames. An image of a log cabin finally appears. The date "1832" is superimposed over the cabin, written in script that resembles sticks or pieces of lumber. Clearly, these are Lincoln's prairie years.

As act 1 begins, Thomas Lincoln, Abe's father, is shown watching a rainstorm through one of the cabin's few windows. Abe's stepmother, Sarah Bush Lincoln, does needlework in a rocking chair. Young Abe reclines lazily on the floor before the fire with a book in hand. As he reads, his father complains of the heavy rain. Annoyed by his son's indifference, the elder Lincoln gripes: "Even if it stopped, you wouldn't notice it. Seein' as how you've everlastin' got your nose stuck in some book!" Lincoln tells his father that the book is "called Shakespeare," which he describes as "kinda poetry." His stepmother suggests that one day he might write poetry—a comment Abe receives with a smile. His father responds, "Over my dead body."

The film's first scene establishes a good deal of context. It is evident immediately that Lincoln came from humble beginnings (the condition of the cabin, his father's colloquial English) and that he was self-educated. However, the meanings that might be derived from this establishing scene are not limited to such easy observations. For instance, Lincoln lore maintains that as a child he once borrowed a book from a library and had to hide it from his disapproving father in a hole in the roof of the family's cabin. One night a rainstorm came, so the tale goes, which soaked the book. Honest Abe worked to pay back the library.

The spectator familiar with this tale from Lincoln's childhood could draw upon it for information regarding Lincoln's character (honesty, integrity, intellectual curiosity), which might figure in his actions later in the film. Additionally, the historical Lincoln is known nearly as much for his proficiency as a writer as for his political accomplishments. Indeed, one Lincoln scholar has referred to the Gettysburg Address as "unforgettable poetry."[22] Thus the brief opening scene of *Abe Lincoln in Illinois* contains multiple opportunities for viewers to draw on their extratextual knowledge of Lincoln's life in order to add content to, and derive further meaning from, the narrative.

However, it is important to note that doing so is not essential at this early stage in order to make sense of the film. Someone completely unfamiliar with Lincoln's life and legend could easily follow the story thus far. This will change. Cromwell's text slowly transitions from one that *permits* the learned viewer to contribute to the story beyond what is provided by the plot to one that *demands* such collaboration.

This opening scene ends when two men arrive to offer Abe the chance to earn $20 a month by taking a flatboat of hogs to New Orleans. "We're starting from a town called Springfield," one of them announces. The audience now knows more than Abe—specifically, that his time in Springfield will not be as brief as he may think. Although Lincoln's father is visibly excited by his son's lucrative opportunity, it is clear that Abe does not share the enthusiasm. Cheerlessly, he says good-bye to his beloved stepmother, whose parting words foreshadow Lincoln's future and articulate one of the film's central themes: "Wherever you go, whatever you do, remember what the Good Book says, 'The world passes, but he that doeth the will of God abideth forever.'" Death and immortality are thus introduced into a film that ends years before Lincoln's assassination and apotheosis.

As with Twain's Huck, Lincoln's jaunt down river is but the first of many journeys to come. One of Lincoln's fellow travelers tries to turn the conversation political: "The last time I was down South they was already talking about annexing the United States. I tell you, these suckers up here, they don't know their own head from an ax handle. Why, I remember one time when—" Here Lincoln interrupts the man in mid-sentence by asking what town they are passing. This moment marks the emergence of an interesting struggle that defines much of the narrative: Lincoln is concerned primarily with present personal matters, while nearly all other characters seem to be pushing him toward future public matters. Very much the reluctant hero, Lincoln will spend much of the film trying to reconcile internal desires with external pressures. Just as in 1939's *Young*

Mr. Lincoln, our hero must negotiate the competing claims of private interest and public duty. But unlike Henry Fonda's Lincoln, whose interest in the law and politics seems to come from something within him, Massey's Lincoln shows little interest in such public matters until they collide with his personal life.

The town they are passing is New Salem, where the flatboat makes an unscheduled stop after accidentally losing much of its cargo in the river. Lincoln and several other men scramble to recover the lost load of hogs. As he lies on the ground wrestling with one of the animals, Lincoln finds himself at the feet of a young woman. The subsequent dialogue features Lincoln's wit.

> Lincoln: My name's Abe Lincoln.
> Rutledge: And mine's Ann Rutledge.
> Lincoln: I don't know the name of the pig.

Rutledge wishes Lincoln luck and he returns to the boat. One of the men traveling with him asks Lincoln if he would like a job in the store he plans to open when they return to New Salem. His eyes fixed on Rutledge on the shore, Lincoln responds, "I sure do."

When Lincoln returns to New Salem it is Election Day, and an old man named Ben Mattling is (literally) on a stump delivering a speech. The crowd is heckling the man who, Lincoln's companion informs him, "makes the same speech every year." Mattling begins, "In the year 1776, we stated the proposition that all men are created equal. And now look at us." The crowd erupts with laughter. Sherwood has acknowledged that Mattling is a product of his imagination, "introduced solely to show that Lincoln knew men who had fought in the Revolution."[23]

Mattling functions within the film in two important ways, each centering on the film's unusual treatment of time. First, by connecting Lincoln to the Founding Fathers, Mattling serves to introduce the image of Lincoln as the First American. This depiction is not as well known as, for example, Honest Abe or the Great Emancipator, but it is still an important part of Lincoln's place in American memory. The Founding Fathers, of course, were British, not American, at least by birth. The image of Lincoln as the First American sees him as the first descendent of the Founding Fathers to have lived and died according to the democratic ideals given voice in the Constitution. More than any other Lincoln film, *Abe Lincoln in Illinois* presents its hero as the direct descendent of the framers of the Constitution and the realization of their vision for the United States.

Second, Mattling's appearance within the narrative further serves to activate the audience's requisite memory work, prompting viewers to see the present through the lens of the past and future. The proposition that Mattling mentions is drawn from the Declaration of Independence, but of course most viewers will associate the expressed ideal with Lincoln's 1863 address at Gettysburg. By foreshadowing yet another event that occurred in Lincoln's post-Illinois years, the film continues to force our attention to a future that lies beyond its narrative horizon.

Jack Armstrong and the rest of the Clary's Grove Boys enter the town tavern, owned by the Rutledge family, and begin to steal alcohol. Ann Rutledge pleads with the men of New Salem to stop them, but none comes forward except Mattling, who is no match for the younger, stronger Armstrong. In this scene Jack Armstrong fulfills the same role as Big Buck in *Young Mr. Lincoln.* In fact, both characters utter a nearly identical line. In *Young Mr. Lincoln,* Big Buck shouts at young Abe, "I'm Big Buck, alright, I'm the biggest buck in this lick!" However, when Lincoln invites him to "come on up and wet your horns," Big Buck declines. In *Abe Lincoln in Illinois,* Jack Armstrong challenges all of New Salem with the words "I'm the big buck in this lick. And any of you wanna wet your horns all you gotta to do is—" At this point Armstrong notices Lincoln and invites him to fight. In Cromwell's film, it is Lincoln who declines the offer—initially. After recognizing Ann Rutledge—that is, after identifying a personal motive for public action—Lincoln challenges Armstrong in front of the whole town. Their clash is more of a wrestling match than a boxing encounter, but eventually Lincoln gets the better of his foe. It is his first public victory.

After Lincoln defeats Armstrong, the men of New Salem try to put Abe "to work for the government." He responds, "I don't want to be no politician." However, when our reluctant hero is assured that all he'll do is help with the counting of ballots—to ensure an honest vote—Lincoln agrees. Public service for its own sake continues to hold little interest for

Lincoln, but ensuring an honest outcome seems to make the endeavor a worthy one. In a low-angle shot that is excessively melodramatic even for a Lincoln film, he raises his right hand and begins to speak the oath: "I, Abraham Lincoln, do solemnly swear to uphold the Constitution of the United States." The scene is followed by a long, slow fade to black during which viewers are again provided sufficient time to ponder the present events in light of those we know to be in Lincoln's future.

So far, the viewer of *Abe Lincoln in Illinois* has witnessed three significant events in Lincoln's early life: his departure from home, his first meeting with Ann Rutledge, and his entry into public life. As we have viewed these events, the film seems to have quite intentionally invited us to draw comparisons with corresponding events in Lincoln's later life: his death in 1865 is evoked by Sarah Bush, his speech at Gettysburg in 1863 is partially mimicked by Ben Mattling, and his recitation of the oath is strikingly similar to his first and second inaugural speeches. To this point, the film has been "deliberately asserting a doubleness of structure, in which the two texts, one forwards and one backwards, exist in simultaneous relation to one another."[24] The film's call to participate in the co-creation of these parallel narratives is sustained throughout, although the structure becomes much more complex as the film progresses.

In act 1, scene 1 of Sherwood's play, Lincoln is shown receiving instruction in composition at the home of Mentor Graham. In a scene now relocated to Lincoln's general store, a significantly condensed version of the exchange as penned by Sherwood unfolds.

> Graham: What's your objection to the city, Abe? Ever seen one?
> Lincoln: Sure. I been down rivers in New Orleans. You know, every minute of the time I was there I was scared. I was scared of people.
> Graham: Did you imagine that they'd rob you of all your gold and your jewels?
> Lincoln: No. I was scared they'd kill me.
> Graham: Why? Why would they want to kill you?
> Lincoln: I don't know.
> Graham: You're a hopeless mess of inconsistency, Abe Lincoln.

The conclusion of the scene serves no direct purpose within the narrative, as the film ends as Lincoln leaves Illinois for Washington, D.C.—well before his assassination. Certainly one could argue that the dialogue reinforces the image of Lincoln as self-educated and reluctant, but the final exchange makes explicit reference to an event only intimated by Sarah Bush in the film's first scene. Further, in the stage play, Lincoln goes on to explain that his preoccupation with death is the result of having lost his mother at an early age. However, in the film, Lincoln's comments about death seem to refer only to his own, and in so doing create a tension that is never resolved on-screen.

Later in the New Salem sequence, Lincoln is told that the Black Hawk War has begun and that the men of New Salem have elected him captain of the First Brigade of Mountain Volunteers. There is no doubt that Lincoln's destiny is very much beyond his control. Always the reluctant hero, Abe protests, "I don't know. It seems to me as if those Indians have a right to their own land." Eventually he is persuaded to fight so that the country might finally settle the Kansas-Nebraska territory and live in peace.

Comic relief follows these serious scenes in the form of a humorous image of Lincoln struggling to lead his troops through basic-training exercises. But for all that is made of Lincoln's entry into this war, viewers are offered no battle scenes, and the outcome of the war is not even mentioned. That Lincoln finally has agreed to fulfill a public duty in which he had no real personal interest seems to be the episode's sole contribution to our understanding of his evolving character. This development will be of use later in our understanding of Lincoln's reluctant acceptance of the presidency.

After the war, Lincoln is appointed New Salem's postmaster, and in that position he delivers to Ann Rutledge a letter from her fiancé in which he calls off their engagement. Already distraught, she realizes that she has no money to pay for the postage. Lincoln assures her, "The government can wait." Lincoln may be in no hurry, but the government is anxious for Lincoln. In the next scene, he is called away from the post office to meet with several men who want him to run for a seat in the Illinois State Assembly. Lincoln leaves a handwritten sign at the post office that reads: "I'll be right back. A. L." Viewers know it to be untrue.

Despite Ben Mattling's earlier advice to stay out of politics, Lincoln eventually agrees to follow in the footsteps of the Founding Fathers. During the meeting, Lincoln gives the men no definitive answer, and he is noticeably distracted by Ann Rutledge, who is serving drinks. When everyone else exits through the front door, Lincoln follows Rutledge through the back door and into the woods where he tries to console her about her broken engagement. Although Lincoln seems sincere in trying to ease her pain and embarrassment, he is not so selfless as to allow an opportunity to court her pass. Cleverly, he offers to keep company with Ann for a while so that the old women in New Salem will not gossip about her. Just as Lincoln gave the men no definitive answer regarding his intentions, Rutledge gives him no direct response regarding hers.

The most interesting aspect of this scene is that it features the only significant development in the first section of the film that is not paralleled by some other event in Lincoln's future. The obvious parallel would seem to be Lincoln's relationship with his future wife, Mary Todd, but because that is portrayed later in the film, there is no need for viewers to look forward to it. Rather, the film will invite us to look back upon this moment later, once the film and its viewers share a past (the film's first section) upon which both can reflect.

Soon all of New Salem is celebrating Lincoln's run for the legislature. After much dancing at a campaign rally, Rutledge faints and is taken away to her home. Meanwhile, Lincoln delivers a brief election night speech. Directly beside him, on the wall of the cabin, is the dark shadow of a man who is presumably listening to the speech from a position off-camera. The man's profile shows his pronounced beard and stovepipe hat—the very image that has come to define Lincoln. The image quite literally foreshadows the man Lincoln is becoming.

When he finishes speaking, Lincoln is told that Ann Rutledge is dying. As New Salem's residents cast their votes for Lincoln, he rushes to Rutledge's side. Rutledge dies without having returned Lincoln's love; she even mistakes him for her fiancé in her final moments. Unlike other films about Lincoln's early life, *Abe Lincoln in Illinois* does not suggest that a romantic relationship ever existed between the two. This time Lincoln's love goes unrequited.

As noted previously, much of the narrative action within this section invites audiences to understand that action both for its own sake and as it stands in relation to Lincoln's life after Illinois. Although this strategy continues in acts 2 and 3, there is a noticeable shift to another level of activity that is now added to an already complex process. The film continues to advance rather obvious invitations to consider its present in relation to Lincoln's future. Less obvious, however, is the manner in which the second and third sections of the film closely resemble the structure rehearsed with viewers in the first section. The film has trained its audience to make certain inferences and to draw certain conclusions based on the development of narrative action in its lengthy first section; the next two sections follow a similar form and in so doing successfully increase the audience's burden of meaning making without resulting in confusion.

Act 2: Springfield, Part I

Lincoln's departure for the legislature is presented as bittersweet. Still mourning Rutledge's death, Lincoln is no more enthusiastic about the parade in his honor than is his friend Judge Bowling Green, who says somberly, "They're coming, Abe." In the following scene, Stephen A. Douglas is shown in the legislature debating the murder of Elijah Lovejoy, an abolitionist newspaper editor who was killed by a proslavery mob. The politicians are unable to lure Lincoln into the discussion. Again we find ourselves comparing Lincoln to the Founding Fathers, who established in the Constitutional Congress the right of a free press, in whose defense Lovejoy was murdered. However, here in act 2, where the hero of a three-act drama usually falters, Lincoln is unable to fulfill the promise of his pedigree. Personal matters have distracted the First American from his public obligation to use the law as a weapon against injustice and oppression.

Announcing his intention not to seek reelection, Lincoln shares a few humorous observations about politics and then quickly takes his leave. We later find Lincoln practicing law in Springfield with partner John Stuart. After being shown the text of an antipolitical letter that Lincoln is composing, William Herndon, with whom Lincoln would later form a new law practice, informs Lincoln that he has earned a very positive reputation in Springfield. However, Lincoln shows no interest in his newfound fame.

The similarities between the opening scenes in acts 1 and 2 are remarkable. In each sequence, Lincoln reluctantly leaves his home and his most significant relationships (with Sarah Bush Lincoln and Ann Rutledge). Lincoln briefly tries his hand at a new job (first on the flatboat, then in the legislature) and refuses to be drawn into a political discussion. He establishes a new home (New Salem and Springfield) and his familiar reputation.

That the beginnings of these sections so clearly mirror one another makes for a compelling (if not conclusive) argument that the first section was intended to prepare viewers to understand the formal structure that the rest of the film follows. But that is not all. Even if we consider just one scene, we can begin to get a sense of the awesome complexity of this remarkable film. The scene in which Lincoln departs for the legislature not only foreshadows the one in which he departs for Washington, D.C., it also reminds us of the scene when Lincoln left Kentucky, which itself foreshadowed Lincoln's death. Lincoln's entire life is, in a sense, laid out here before us in but a few seconds of the film—provided we are able to see it.

Temporarily out of politics, Lincoln attends a party where he meets Mary Todd. The scene is quite similar in form and content to the political rally at which Ann Rutledge fainted, with one noticeable exception: now Lincoln is pursued rather than pursuing. The similarities in the content of these scenes—dancing, political discussions, Lincoln's effective use of humor—set them apart from the rest of the film and suggest that viewers are invited to contrast Lincoln's new relationship with his old one. The scene also prepares viewers, quite conspicuously, for a critical moment in the film's final section: Lincoln's debates with Stephen A. Douglas.

At the party, Lincoln gets the better of Douglas in a friendly contest of wits in the presence of Mary Todd, after which Douglas utters, "Something tells me I shouldn't have started this." Repetitions abound in this part of the film. Lincoln's conversation with Todd at the party is obviously similar to his conversation with Rutledge in the woods of New Salem. Afterward, William Herndon and Bowling Green encourage Lincoln to run for Congress, just as he had been encouraged by other men to run for the legislature. Although not every scene in the film's second section gestures back to another in the first section, so many of them do that even if it was not an intentional design it would have an effect on the viewer's experience of the film.

Still a reluctant hero, Lincoln declines to run for Congress. "I am opposed to slavery," he assures Green, "but I'm even more opposed to getting myself into trouble." As Green and Herndon resume their efforts, Lincoln moves to the window of the law office as his attention is drawn to Mary Todd, who is passing through the streets of Springfield below. The moment is interesting because it may be the only one in the film in which Lincoln seems genuinely drawn to his future wife. Although he will later propose marriage, he seems at that moment more like a man accepting destiny than a man pursuing love. This scene reminds the viewer of several others in which Lincoln watched Rutledge through doorways and windows with similar interest.

After a slow fade to black, during which time Lincoln's relationship with Todd seems to have intensified greatly, Todd announces to her family that she intends to marry Lincoln. Unenthusiastic, to say the least, her sister pleads with her not to condemn herself to such a "narrow life." Undeterred, Todd declares: "I'm ready to fight to make him fulfill his destiny." The scene is brief but significant. At this point in the film the personal and the political finally collide. Lincoln's love for Rutledge provided at least a distraction, if not a kind a refuge, from the demands of public life. Although he was on occasion persuaded to involve himself in public matters, those efforts were short-lived. But eventually Todd's ambition and Lincoln's affection (if we can call it that) for her will set him on a path from which he will not have the opportunity to stray.

Springfield's most prominent men toast Lincoln's engagement to Todd in the local saloon. However, Lincoln confesses to Josh Speed and William Herndon that he cannot go through with the marriage. Despite Herndon's pleas that Lincoln marry Todd and enter politics "for the slaves," Lincoln departs. After a transitional shot in which Springfield's seasons change, we find Lincoln walking New Salem's deserted streets. This scene, which Sherwood called "the most completely fictitious" in the whole story, marks the turning point in the film.[25] It was during his trip back to New Salem that the Lincoln in Sherwood's play uttered the prayer that, as Massey saw it, explained his dramatic change of heart. Having omitted the prayer from the film version, Sherwood and Cromwell had to convey that transformation by other means. After walking through the empty tavern in which he was first called into politics, Lincoln pauses at the back door, just as he did so long ago before professing his love to Rutledge. Here the film takes great license: looking over Lincoln's shoulder, viewers actually see what at first glance appears to be the ghost of Ann Rutledge walking through the woods. Lincoln's calm demeanor assures us that what we are seeing is not truly a specter but rather a projection of his thoughts and memories.

Bruce F. Kawin calls this uncommon form of narration "mindscreen," wherein the camera presents for the viewer not only what a character says or sees but what that character thinks.[26] As Lincoln moves to the very tree near which he and Rutledge shared their most intimate exchange, his thoughts drift back to the words of another woman that he dearly loved. Again those thoughts are made known to the film's viewers as we hear the words Sarah Bush spoke when Lincoln last saw her: "The world passes, but he that doeth the will of God abideth forever." This one simple statement captures the essence of Lincoln's entire life as well as the timeless place that he has come to occupy in death.

Now character and viewer are ready for him to accept his destiny. Lincoln returns to Springfield and for the second time proposes marriage to Todd. Said Sherwood of Lincoln's proposal: "All that can be said about this brief scene is that it seemed necessary. . . . Lincoln's return to Mary Todd is merely expressive of his acceptance of his destiny."[27]

Act 3: Springfield, Part II

The film's third and final section begins with a montage that depicts Lincoln's rise to national prominence along with the nation's initial rise but subsequent decline. Superimposed over the montage are the words "And then—years that marked the growth of a man, and a nation." By the end of the sequence, it is clear that Lincoln has fared far better than his country, which now is deeply divided by slavery.

The following scene is one of only a handful in which Lincoln does not appear. Handcuffed to a post in the engine house at Harper's Ferry, the abolitionist John Brown predicts as he is arrested by Lieutenant Colonel Robert E. Lee that the evil of slavery "can be purged from this guilty world only with blood." The scene ends with Brown holding his dying son, whose last words are "It's no use, Pa, you gotta give in to 'em. Somebody else has gotta finish this job." No version of this scene appeared in Sherwood's stage play, but in the film it provides motivation for Lincoln's sudden passion for politics and his commitment to the abolitionist cause.

The legendary Lincoln-Douglas debates occur next. Lincoln's statements in the debates are, Sherwood admits, "a patchwork of quotations and paraphrases from various speeches given by him during the debates and before them and after them, and some of it is from his letters."[28] What seems to be important here is providing Lincoln a forum in which to articulate forcefully his opposition to slavery. However, the scene accomplishes more in its effect on the audience. Viewers are encouraged to continue the memory work they have been engaged in for most of the film, in this case recalling the various sources from which Lincoln's rhetoric has been drawn.

Another montage follows the debates, after the New York newspaper editor Horace Greeley announces that he will write an editorial about "a man named Lincoln." The sequence offers proof of Lincoln's rise to national prominence through images of the many newspaper articles devoted to his speeches. In a subsequent scene, party bosses discuss the possibility of nominating Lincoln as the Whig Party's presidential candidate. After concluding not only that Lincoln would make a suitable candidate but that he would be easy to control, the men agree that his nomination is certain.

Like that other election night in New Salem so many years ago, when his first political victory rang hollow because of Rutledge's death, Lincoln is again distracted by the woman in his life. On the night of the presidential election, Todd allows the stress of the evening to get the best of her, and she eventually scolds Lincoln for joking with members of his campaign team at such an important time. Once the two are alone, Lincoln orders her, in a tone we have not yet heard in the film, never to behave so again. This politician might not be as easy to control as some had thought. Todd leaves before the results are in; although she is present at the rail station in the film's last scene, she does not speak to anyone, including Lincoln, after this argument.

The remainder of the election night scene is devoted to demonstrating Lincoln's apathy toward the contest. After hearing that victory seems certain, Lincoln laments, "Yes, we've fought the good fight—in the dirtiest campaign in the history of corrupt politics. And if I win, I must fill all the dishonest pledges made in my name." Once Lincoln departs, it falls on Herndon to remind viewers what lies ahead for their hero. Speaking to one of the campaign advisors, who acts as something of a stand-in for viewers, Herndon delivers an impassioned speech: "Don't you realize that they've raised ten thousand volunteers in South Carolina? They're arming them! The governor has issued a proclamation saying that if Mr. Lincoln is elected, the state will secede tomorrow, and every other state south of the Dixon Line will go with it. Can you see what that means? War! Civil war! And he'll have the whole terrible responsibility for it—a man who has never wanted anything in his life but to be let alone, in peace!"

Having thus foreshadowed the Civil War, there is but one great event to evoke—Lincoln's assassination. This is soon accomplished when a Captain Kavanagh insists that he and his soldiers escort Lincoln from the building after the election results are in because threats have been made on his life.

The film's final scene, in which Lincoln is shown for the first time with a full beard, depicts the president-elect's famous departure at Springfield's train station. With a blanket drawn over his shoulders, Lincoln appears to have aged considerably since the election. After exchanging a few kind words with former foe Stephen A. Douglas, Lincoln boards the train as the sizable crowd demands a speech. Although the speech delivered by Massey in the play differs significantly from this one, it too seems to be what Sherwood called "a blend of several of Lincoln's utterances."[29]

> No one, not in my situation, can appreciate my feelings of sadness at this parting. To this place, and the kindness of you people, I owe everything. I now leave, not knowing when or whether ever I may return. It is a grave duty which I now face. . . . We gained democracy, and there is now doubt whether it is fit to survive. I have heard of an

> eastern monarch who once charged his wise men to invent him a sentence which should be true and appropriate at all times and situations. They presented him with the words, "And this too shall pass away." That's a comforting thought in times of affliction—"And this too shall pass away." And yet, let us believe that it is not true. Let us live to prove that we can cultivate the natural world around us, and the intellectual and moral world that is within us, so that we may secure an individual, social, and political prosperity, whose course shall be forward, and which, while this earth endures, shall not pass away. I commend you to the care of the Almighty, as I hope in your prayers you may remember me. Friends, one and all, I must now bid you an affectionate farewell.

It is clear from the manner in which the speech is filmed, with its close-up on Lincoln's face as he twice utters the line "This too shall pass away," that he understands the double meaning of his words. Lincoln suspects what viewers already know: that the Union will be preserved at the cost of his life. But if, as Sarah Bush Lincoln predicted earlier in the film, "He that doeth the will of God abideth forever," then Lincoln will never pass away because his memory, like that of the Founding Fathers, shall abide forever. And lest any viewer be left unconvinced of this, the film's closing chorus announces: "His soul goes marching on."

Abe Lincoln in Illinois is a fascinating film. Although *Young Mr. Lincoln* remains the more popular version of Lincoln's youth, the story that Sherwood brought first to the stage and then to the screen is equally sophisticated in its structure and challenging in the demands it places on its audience. Film narration almost always requires the compression of time and space, and that compression is all the more inevitable in the case of a historical film, whose drama will always be only part of the story. What makes *Abe Lincoln in Illinois* an interesting rhetorical text is the manner in which the film exploits this inevitability for its own purposes. Quite self-consciously and reflexively, the film invites its viewers to make sense of its narrative action in relation to its many absences.

As viewers begin to engage in this work, responding to cues to supplement its scenes, the film is preparing them to extend and expand that work on yet another level. Through the film's repetitive structure, viewers are called upon to engage in memory work throughout the experience, recalling what occurred both *earlier* in the film and *later* in history. Cromwell's film thus swirls within a larger narrative that does not end with the film's final frame.

The temporal nature of the interpretive work that the film requires is complemented by the temporal context in which its Lincoln is ultimately defined. Beginning with the introduction of a Revolutionary War veteran and ending with the music over which the closing credits roll—"His soul goes marching on"—*Abe Lincoln in Illinois* presents Lincoln as the First American, direct descendent of the Founding Fathers and enduring symbol of democracy for future generations. In this sense, the film presents Lincoln in a manner very similar to its treatment of Lincoln's story: as transcending time itself. Both the story of *Abe Lincoln in Illinois* and its hero exist in the present while also resonating with America's past and future.

6

Honest Abe

Sandburg's Lincoln (1974–1976)

> Carl Sandburg's *Abraham Lincoln: The Prairie Years and The War Years* is, for better or worse, the best-selling, most widely read, and most influential book about Lincoln.
>
> —James Hurt, "Sandburg's *Lincoln* within History"

> The sentimental style seeks a total control over consciousness; that is its principal defining characteristic.
>
> —Edwin Black, "The Sentimental Style as Escapism"

Lincoln's first appearance in Hollywood, in the Edison Film Company's production of *Uncle Tom's Cabin* (1903), was a simple and sentimental depiction of a complex man. Thus began a century of representation on the big screen. In the second half of the twentieth century, Lincoln would make several important appearances on the small screen—at least one of them every bit as sentimental as his film debut.

Beginning in the 1970s, the often melodramatic made-for-television miniseries became a popular cultural form, and by the late 1980s, Abraham Lincoln emerged as one of its brightest stars. *Sandburg's Lincoln* is an overly sentimental text that acted as a kind of anti-activist antidote for mid-1970s television audiences, weary after a decade of protest and upheaval. Airing in the years leading up to the nation's bicentennial celebration, *Sandburg's Lincoln* offered Americans a look back in time through a sentimental lens that required them to do no more than celebrate Lincoln's personal qualities and their own public commitments. The miniseries gave Americans permission to feel good again precisely by giving them absolutely nothing about which to feel bad.

The six-part television adaptation of Sandburg's best-selling biographies—*Abraham Lincoln: The Prairie Years* and *Abraham Lincoln: The War Years*—presented Lincoln in many contexts, but none was as explicitly promoted as Lincoln's wholesome image as Honest Abe. After a decade of governmental machinations and deception that involved, among other issues, Vietnam and Watergate, *Sandburg's Lincoln* offered America a national hero whose personal strength and political success were the direct result of his integrity and righteousness.

Lincoln Divided

The entertainment industry had tried before to bring Lincoln to life in serial fashion. And it had failed. Twice. Benjamin Chapin's *Lincoln Cycle* in the 1910s was an early and admirably ambitious effort to create a whole series of feature-length films that would document Lincoln's life from birth to death. After some initial success, Chapin's magnum opus ultimately failed, due to a lack of funds, decreasing support from the community of film critics, and ultimately his own untimely death.

Abraham Lincoln: The Early Years was a series of five half-hour episodes that aired on CBS between 1952 and 1953. The series did for television what Chapin and *The Lincoln Cycle* had tried to do for movies. The complete series was written by James Agee, who had recently written the script for *The African Queen* and who would soon go on to write *The Night of the Hunter.* As the title of the series suggests, individual episodes focus primarily on Lincoln's early years in Kentucky, Indiana, and Illinois. Collectively they present a Lincoln who is "socially-awkward, but people are drawn to him because of his intellect, kindness and sense of humor." One Lincoln scholar concludes that Royal Dano, who portrays Lincoln, "gives a tremendous performance," and that "Agee's script is a masterpiece."[1]

Perhaps the most important consequence of *Abraham Lincoln: The Early Years* is that it started a serious public discussion about the memory work performed by popular culture. So much so, in fact, that CBS eventually aired a debate between Agee and a historian from Columbia University.[2] The debate is said to have focused on the series' inclusion of Lincoln's alleged relationship with Ann Rutledge. However, more important than the specific details of the debate is the fact that the debate took place at all—a clear sign that Americans were taking seriously the role of movies and miniseries in shaping their collective past.

Sandburg's Lincoln

The 1970s saw yet another revival of interest in Lincoln on television. As 1976 drew closer and America prepared to celebrate its bicentennial, the country began once again to take stock of itself and its heroes. Lincoln, naturally, resurfaced as the enduring symbol of all that is great about America. By some accounts, no fewer than nineteen movies, miniseries, documentaries, television episodes, and educational shorts aired between 1970 and 1976.[3] *Sandburg's Lincoln* was unquestionably the most important Lincoln project of the decade, and it remains among the most interesting ever filmed. Unfortunately, few people have seen it since its initial broadcast because the series remains extremely difficult to find on DVD or online, unlike *Gore Vidal's Lincoln* (1988), which remains widely available. Thus the effect *Sandburg's Lincoln* had on the collective memory of Lincoln seems to be limited to the cultural work of remembrance that it accomplished leading up to the 1976 bicentennial.

The writer Carl Sandburg was born in Illinois in the decade after the Civil War. Like Lincoln, his education was sporadic, and most of his life would be spent in the Midwest. The three-time Pulitzer winner had an impact in nearly every conceivable genre of both fiction and nonfiction, including as a journalist, reviewer, children's author, poet, biographer, historian, and essayist. His definitive work remains his two-volume Lincoln biography, *Abraham Lincoln: The Prairie Years* (1926), and *Abraham Lincoln: The War Years* (1939).

Sandburg wrote as the voice of America's conscience, and his writings on the president quickly became the definitive works on Lincoln's life. Although they are now regarded as sentimental portraits, not taken seriously as critical biographies, his two Lincoln books defined the man for much of the twentieth century, and they continue to exert an influence on the public today. Writing in the *Journal of the Abraham Lincoln Association,* James Hurt likely speaks for many academic historians when he laments that "more Americans have learned their Lincoln from Sandburg than from any other source" and that Sandburg's work "has had an enormous impact on popular conceptions of Lincoln."[4]

In *Sandburg's Lincoln,* the accomplished stage actor Hal Holbrook portrayed Lincoln in a role he would later reprise in the miniseries *North and South* (1985) and *North and South: Book II* (1986). Unlike most actors who play Lincoln, Holbrook wore extensive makeup to transform his appearance, and he altered his voice tremendously. The effect rendered the star almost unrecognizable, but it achieved a sense of authenticity not found in other films, which were essentially star vehicles. The series was directed by television veteran George Schaefer, and the many writers who contributed to the adaptation included Jerome Lawrence and Robert E. Lee, best known for their play *Inherit the Wind.* The executive producer was television icon David L. Wolper, whose specialty was the production of television content of historical and social significance—in 1977 he made television history with his remarkable miniseries *Roots.*

Sandburg's Lincoln is a series in six episodes, each one hour long, all shown on NBC between 1974 and 1976. The series' emphasis was decidedly on Lincoln's war years, as only one episode dealt with what Sandburg had called Lincoln's prairie years. Oddly, the episodes as aired did not present a chronological retelling of Lincoln's life. Instead, they offered apparently random snapshots of the man at various moments during his life. "Producing and premiering the series with no regard to chronological order might seem like a strange decision, but it likely did not cause a great deal of viewer confusion because the episodes aired as special presentations irregularly over a two-year period. Also, each episode offered storylines that were resolved by the end of that particular episode's running time, so they could be enjoyed individually as well as collectively. At any rate, the series did have the good sense to conclude by airing 'The Last Days' as its sixth and final episode in April 1976."[5]

In the following analysis, each episode is analyzed in the order in which it appeared to television audiences, not as the events depicted actually occurred more than a century prior. The goal is to read the series as it revealed itself—and Lincoln—to American audiences preparing to celebrate the anniversary of the nation that Lincoln had preserved.

Episode 1: "Mrs. Lincoln's Husband"

The first episode, "Mrs. Lincoln's Husband," premiered on NBC in September 1974. The episode examines the Lincolns' notoriously difficult marriage, emphasizing the extent to which it was strained during the long and difficult Civil War. It was, quite frankly, an odd place to begin a national narrative. The next episode would not air until February of the following year, meaning that for five months this unusual portrait of Lincoln's unhappy home life would stand alone in the minds of American television viewers, who were supposed to be getting excited about the coming bicentennial.

Rarely is Mary Todd Lincoln treated favorably by the historical community, and those who have sought to dramatize the Lincolns' marriage on the stage and screen have been especially tough on her. Whether or not she deserves such treatment, Mary is nearly always depicted as ambitious to the point of being calculating, and difficult to the point of being delusional.[6] Indeed, if Stephen Douglas is cast as Lincoln's main nemesis in depictions of the prairie years, it is the president's own wife with whom he must do battle during the war years.

The episode concentrates on the Lincolns' relationship, in particular the stress caused by the war and the devastating loss of their young son, Willie. Observed one writer, "The hour doesn't contain a plot, exactly, just a series of events that serve to illustrate and illuminate the Lincolns' marriage."[7] Mary is depicted as struggling under the weight of her duties as First Lady, and Lincoln as having yet one more difficult responsibility with which to deal. In a sense, it is more Mary's story than Abe's.

The hour begins with a picture of familial bliss: the Lincolns are enjoying a leisurely breakfast during which they playfully tease one another. The mood does not last. As Lincoln is pulled away to deal with news about the war, Mary speaks with her children. Here she demonstrates that she is thoughtful and articulate and empathetic—not at all the qualities traditionally ascribed to her by Hollywood screenwriters. The scene is complicated by the anticipated arrival of Mary's sister, whose husband was recently killed in the war. Lincoln's advisors warn him about the potential political fallout of hosting the widow of a Confederate soldier, but Lincoln disregards the advice. In fact, he makes matters worse for himself by inviting Charles Sherwood Stratton, better known as General Tom Thumb, to a formal gathering at the White House. Stratton was a famous performer in P. T. Barnum's circus, standing just over three feet in height, who really did meet President Lincoln at the White House. In this episode, many of the guests at the event are shocked and offended that Lincoln would host sideshow performers while the war rages on. In fact, Lincoln's own son Robert refuses to attend a party at which "freaks" will be present.

If all of this seems like an odd context for the first episode of *Sandburg's Lincoln,* it is. However, the whole scene permits the miniseries to demonstrate Mary's many positive qualities. She scolds her son for his intolerance and defends her sister's presence at the party. Although Mary is a political liability—unpopular among some of Lincoln's supporters because she is a Southerner and because of her extravagant spending—she is here presented as a principled defender of all who surround her. Although many people in Washington suspect that she is a spy for the South, Mary is portrayed as a loving wife and mother.

When their young son Willie dies from an illness, both Lincolns are naturally distraught. Still, even as she grieves, Mary maintains her dignity and compassion; she does not descend into madness as in many other portrayals. Whereas most of Hollywood's Mary Todd Lincolns are infected from within, *Sandburg's Lincoln* represents her as a sympathetic victim of too many tragic circumstances. One critic concluded: "This Mary is not insane, nor a harpy; just a woman battered by self-doubts and the suspicions of others. Abe comforts and compliments her; they are by far the most affectionate Lincolns in film."[8] They are indeed represented as uncommonly close, and Mary as uncommonly composed. In this sense, *Sandburg's Lincoln* began in a strange place and in a strange way—and it quickly moved on to places stranger still.

Episode 2: "Sad Figure Laughing"

Aired in February 1975, the second episode in the series coincided with the annual celebration of Lincoln's birth. The episode pits Lincoln against his secretary of the treasury, Salmon P. Chase, as his bid for reelection nears. Of all the possible areas of Lincoln's life in which one might find drama, Lincoln's tense relationship with Chase was an odd choice indeed. It hardly seems to qualify as one of the major moments in Lincoln's life. Consider that the Emancipation Proclamation is hardly mentioned in the series, and here we have one of only six episodes devoted to Salmon P. Chase.

In fairness, the episode does cover the run-up to Lincoln's all-important reelection in 1864. In addition, given Chase's strong support for the abolitionist movement, the focus on his character introduces the issue of slavery early in the series. Chase was far more radical in his antislavery views than Lincoln. This distinction is emphasized in the opening scene when one of Chase's supporters asks about Lincoln, "Why didn't he emancipate the slaves as soon as the war started? Why didn't he free them all?" No doubt these are questions that most Americans have asked themselves about their beloved Lincoln, and Chase's presence permits the series to tackle them head-on. The episode offers a clear answer midway through the story, when Lincoln assures Chase that preserving the Union is his top priority and that freeing all of the slaves would have made that impossible. As Lincoln puts it, "We'll do away with slavery. It'll happen sure as sunrise. But I want to make sure there's a country left for those poor people to be free in."

Chase was an unusual choice as a central figure in the retelling of Lincoln's life, even in a miniseries that was cosponsored by the American Bankers Association. That said, the contrast between the two men was classically cinematic. According to Hugh McCulloch, who followed Chase as secretary of the treasury after President Lincoln nominated Chase for a seat on the Supreme Court, Lincoln and Chase "were about as unlike in appearance, in education, manners, in taste, and temperament, as two eminent men could be."[9]

The episode opens in 1864 with Chase and his daughter scheming to wrestle the Republican Party nomination away from the incumbent Lincoln. Lincoln is not at all enthusiastic about a second term, but he feels that he cannot abandon the nation during wartime. Chase is represented as sincerely respecting the president. However, Chase's commitment to total abolition inspires him to compete for the nomination. Another element of Chase's concern is that Lincoln's continual use of humor has damaged his ability to lead. The episode is titled "Sad Figure Laughing" in reference to Lincoln's legendary use of humor to endear himself to friends and to induce his enemies to underestimate him.

Lincoln, of course, secures the nomination. He refuses to accept Chase's offer to resign as secretary of the treasury, permitting the series to present evidence of Lincoln's conciliatory tendencies. In fact, after Lincoln wins the election, he nominates Chase to be the next chief justice of the U.S. Supreme Court. The gesture foreshadows Lincoln's treatment of the South after Lee's surrender and the end of the Civil War. And of his tendency to tell humorous stories in the saddest of situations, Lincoln explains it with these simple words: "If I could not get a momentary respite from the burden I am constantly carrying, I'm afraid my heart would break."

Episode 3: "Prairie Lawyer"

The third episode aired in April 1975, the month in which Lincoln lovers observe the anniversaries of the start of the Civil War and the assassination of Lincoln. It was in this commemorative context that audiences watched "Prairie Lawyer," the only episode to cover Lincoln's life before politics. It is also the episode that defined this Lincoln as, primarily, Honest Abe. After the two unusual stories about Mary Todd and Salmon P. Chase, in which no clear identity had been established for Lincoln, episode 3 gave its audience a most familiar hero.

The episode is set in Springfield during Lincoln's career as a lawyer, and it features his friendly rivalry with Stephen A. Douglas. Although the episode has been faulted because its "treatment of certain historical facts leaves much to be desired," it at least addresses a part of Lincoln's life rarely mentioned by other Lincoln films: Lincoln's relationship with Mary Owens.[10] Unlike Lincoln's relationship with Ann Rutledge, which remains undocumented, Lincoln's involvement with Mary Owens is beyond doubt. Their relationship, however, was apparently both brief and awkward, which may be why Hollywood has tended to avoid it altogether.

After convincing Owens to move from Kentucky to Illinois so that he might court her, the historical Lincoln discovered that she was not what he remembered, and that he was not the least bit interested in her. As he later wrote to a friend, "I knew she was over-size, but she now appeared a fair match for Falstaff."[11] As one might imagine, *Sandburg's Lincoln* does not emphasize this fact, instead presenting Lincoln as conflicted about whether or not he wants to marry any woman, not just Mary Owens. A simple lack of attraction, then, was replaced by Sandburg with a more acceptable sense of duty and destiny, one that is fulfilled at the end of the episode when Lincoln meets his future wife, Mary Todd.

The episode opens with Lincoln lore turned on its ear. Lincoln discovers that he will be opposing Stephen A. Douglas, though not in a campaign. He and Douglas will be on opposite sides of a murder trial, with Lincoln defending the accused. Meanwhile, it is Lincoln's law partner, John Stuart, who is running against Douglas for Congress, and of course it seems to be the wrong Mary—Owens, not Todd—who has caught Lincoln's eye. Amid all the confusion this must have caused viewers who thought they knew Lincoln's life nearly as well as their own, the episode moves quickly to the dilemma around which it is to center: Lincoln's cold feet.

As the episode represents the event, it is not Owens's appearance that changes Lincoln's heart. Rather, he seems opposed to the idea of marrying anyone. After agreeing to make good on his offer of marriage, Lincoln proceeds to discourage Mary from accepting. Oddly, when Mary Owens does eventually turn him down, Lincoln seems genuinely disappointed.

After initially believing that his client may be guilty of premeditated murder, Honest Abe is relieved to find that the case is not so simple. First he convinces the court to delay the murder trial until after the election so that Douglas's political ambitions will not become entangled with his role in this very visible court case. After Lincoln stumps for Stuart with the sort of speech that is typically featured in Lincoln films as part of one of his own campaigns, viewers learn that Douglas has been defeated.

The episode finally moves on to the trial. Lincoln argues persuasively that his client acted in self-defense. As he awaits the jury's decision, Lincoln is let off the hook by Mary Owens. His client is also let off the hook when the jury decides in his favor. That night, Lincoln attends a dance where he is introduced to Mary Todd, an attractive young woman with whom he dances "in the worst way."

It is clear even to the casual viewer that the episode invites a comparison between Lincoln's handling of the engagement and his management of the trial. Although he eventually triumphs in both arenas, as viewers suspect he will, his straightforward tactics in the courtroom serve him far better than his crooked strategy in his courtship. To judge and jury, Honest Abe speaks from the heart and thus wins with relative ease. But his arguably manipulative handling of Mary Owens makes that case far more difficult to win. From this point forward, it is Honest Abe who stars in *Sandburg's Lincoln.*

Episode 4: "The Unwilling Warrior"

"The Unwilling Warrior" appeared a full year after the series debuted with "Mrs. Lincoln's Husband." This fourth installment, rather than concentrating on a minor episode in Lincoln's life, spanned his whole presidency. As the title suggests, the focus was on Lincoln as commander in chief and on the progress of the Civil War. This was, in many respects, the payoff that followed a year's worth of buildup—the visualization of that part of Lincoln's life that the audience likely had been waiting to see and for which it had been prepared by the preceding episodes.

Indeed, up to this point, *Sandburg's Lincoln* had been mostly melodrama, not entirely unlike an evening soap opera for history buffs. This was not unexpected, given the style and tone of Sandburg's writings on Lincoln and in light of the generic tendencies of the television miniseries. However, this episode boasted a level of historical realism and authenticity that the previous episodes had lacked. The episode begins where *Vidal's Lincoln* also does, with Honest Abe in disguise sneaking into Washington, D.C., amid concerns that he might be killed before taking the oath of office. The tone of this sequence—and of the episode as a whole—is markedly different from all that has preceded it.

The episode opens with a band of would-be assassins drawing straws to see who will kill "the baboon" before he gets to Washington. Guarded by Pinkerton detectives, Lincoln arrives safely at the White House. He solidifies his stance as an "unwilling warrior" almost immediately: "As I see it, I was elected to be president, not a commander in chief." But of course he must and will be both, eventually becoming the quintessential war president. There is little doubt that the episode would have resonated with Vietnam in the minds of it audience.

Lieutenant Elmer Ellsworth figures significantly in the episode, just as he does in *Gore Vidal's Lincoln*. Ellsworth was a close family friend of the Lincolns and the first casualty of the war, shot while removing a Confederate flag from the rooftop of a hotel across the Potomac from the White House in Alexandria, Virginia. His death is often represented as the incident that made the war personal for Lincoln. In this retelling, it is especially personal because it is Lincoln's son Tad who first spies the rebel flag, planting the seed in Ellsworth's mind that it must be removed lest the Confederates be allowed to insult the new president.

The episode emphasizes Lincoln's unprecedented use of the telegraph as a weapon of war. Ironically, the first message he receives is a report of Ellsworth's death. The emotional impact the news has on Lincoln strengthens his resolve to end the war as quickly as possible. But the war will not be short—the fighting will drag on into his second term in office.

Later in the episode, Lincoln must make the difficult decision to replace General George B. McClellan, whose courage infamously left him outside of Richmond, with General Ulysses S. Grant, who quickly takes Richmond and eventually wins the war. Although the episode is dominated by tense scenes in the president's Cabinet room, it also features re-created battles. "One of the most memorable sequences in this episode," Mark S. Reinhart notes, "is the realistic depiction of Lincoln's visit to the fallen Confederate capital of Richmond in early 1865, only days before Gen. Lee's surrender to Gen. Grant at Appomattox Court House."[12] The episode ends as the president declares, "It's over." Indeed, the war is over, but two episodes remain in this unusual miniseries.

Episode 5: "Crossing Fox River"

In a strange chronological rearrangement, *Sandburg's Lincoln* followed its account of the Civil War by traveling back in time to Lincoln's election in 1860. The episode, which aired in January 1976, dramatizes the messy nomination process and Honest Abe's sincere discomfort with the unethical backroom dealings of the party bosses who ultimately nominate him. For a country that had only recently emerged from the Watergate scandal, this was an especially timely and relevant issue to address.

The episode begins in Springfield as Lincoln accepts the Republican Party's official nomination. He quickly stuns the party bosses when he announces that he does not intend to mount a traveling campaign, and in fact he refuses to speak at all on his own behalf. "Every time I get up to speak," he tells the men who have secured his nomination, "the papers, the others, they'll twist what I say, and make me seem to say what I did not, what I would not." Honesty matters more to this Lincoln than the presidency itself.

The plan works, of course, and Lincoln is elected, but he soon finds himself in conflict with his campaign managers over the process of selecting his Cabinet. They want Lincoln to make good on the many promises they made in order to get him elected. Lincoln wants the best man for each job, not the one who secured the most votes. It is a true moral dilemma.

Mary Lincoln is the first to express concern over what will become of her husband and family as they move to Washington amid rumors of Southern secession and the possibility of civil war. Lincoln slowly begins to share her apprehensions, later telling his law partner, "If I live I'll be back, and we'll go right on practicing just as if nothing had ever happened. I shudder when I think what's ahead." The whole affair is filled with anticipation of the difficulties to come. Unlike his portrayal in some previous episodes, this is a Lincoln whom audiences have seen many times before. He is here the reluctant but willing warrior, aware that he will likely not return from Washington but conceding to go anyway.

The end of the episode overlaps with the beginning of the previous episode, "The Unwilling Warrior." However, if the timeline merges, the details are not redundant. No mention is made of Lincoln sneaking into Washington in disguise, and when Mary stumbles upon hate mail threatening Lincoln's life, both she and the president appear more keenly aware of the dangers that await him than they did upon their arrival in episode 4. The program concludes with Lincoln delivering a portion of his inaugural address and taking the oath of office.

Episode 6: "The Last Days"

The final episode dealt, appropriately, with Lincoln's assassination. It aired on the 111th anniversary of his death, just three months before the nation's bicentennial was to be observed. As such, it negotiated a delicate balance between commemoration and celebration, joy and grief.

The episode begins with the citizens of Washington, D.C., celebrating the end of the war. Set in the peaceful days just after the hard-fought and bloody Civil War, the episode drips with dramatic irony. This Lincoln knows not yet what is coming, but of course the audience knows all too well. This final episode seems to demonstrate that all the tensions shown in previous episodes have been resolved, that all the battles have been won. The Lincolns are at peace with one another, Lincoln has been reelected, the war is over, and the South is being welcomed back.

Lincoln makes clear his intention to treat the South with compassion, which frustrates his supporters in the North and does little to assuage his enemies in the South. Lincoln's Cabinet members are especially frustrated by the president's refusal to punish the South, but he intends to win Southerners over with a carefully developed plan for harmonious reconstruction. As he tells one of his advisors, "For once, I have time. I have time." That evening, Lincoln dreams of his own death, a scene also filmed in *Gore Vidal's Lincoln*. The manner of death is not clear to him, but he dreams of a black coffin in the White House, and he is told in the dream that the box contains the remains of "the president." Later recounting the vision, Lincoln states, "Although it was only a dream, somehow this thing has taken possession of me."

The tone of the episode shifts here from celebratory to somber, but although death threats appear daily in the mail, Lincoln remains optimistic. He tells his Cabinet not of his nightmare but of another dream, one that the audience does not experience. This is a dream Lincoln claims to have had many times before, always followed by a major victory in the war. In the dream, Lincoln says, he is sailing aboard a large vessel, toward "some distant shore," and he knows the vision is a sign of good things to come. With that, he takes his leave to prepare for an evening at the theater.

Although it would seem that Lincoln is no longer concerned for his personal welfare, alone in his study he recites the first line of a William Knox poem whose first stanza reads:

> Oh! why should the spirit of mortal be proud?
> Like a swift-fleeting meteor, a fast-flying cloud,
> A flash of the lightning, a break of the wave,
> Man passeth from life to his rest in the grave.

In the carriage on the way to the theater the president and his wife talk pleasantly about what their lives will be like when they are done with politics, including all the places to which they will travel: California, Europe, the Holy Land. It is not clear if they really believe what they are saying, or if each is pretending for the sake of the other.

The episode ends with our view of the carriage heading toward the theater. Unlike *Gore Vidal's Lincoln,* this miniseries does not show Lincoln's assassination. Rather, it ends with these words on the screen: "That night Abraham Lincoln was assassinated. The prairie years, the war years were over."

Sandburg's Sentiment

If it is possible to sum up in just one word the style of both *Sandburg's Lincoln* and the popular books upon which it was based, that word is *sentimental.* Like all sentimental texts, this one privileges emotion over reason and celebrates the inherent goodness of humanity, in this case represented by Honest Abe. *Sandburg's Lincoln* is, in other words, a melodramatic whitewashing of the historical record—but that is hardly rare in the genre of Lincoln films. In fact, it is the norm.

What made this particular sentimental whitewashing unusually important was its timing. Airing in the wake of the turbulent 1960s, a decade marked by political assassinations, social unrest, another controversial war and, perhaps most significantly, the struggle for civil rights, *Sandburg's Lincoln* offered weary Americans what appeared to be an opportunity to heal their wounds without having to leave their living rooms. Rather than issue a political call for a continuation of the ideological agenda with which Lincoln had come to be associated—especially considering the extent to which the civil rights movement had successfully appropriated Lincoln's image and ethos—the miniseries permitted viewers simply to feel good about Lincoln and about themselves, without asking them to do anything beyond watch and feel.[13]

The sentimental style is common in the culture of nostalgia and is closely associated with Lincoln's century. As Edwin Black notes, "There is no question that in the nineteenth century, at least, in America and in England, at least, there flourished something that can properly be called the sentimental style." This rhetorical style is found most readily and abundantly in the culture of oratory that defined that century, but it did not end with it. Black argues: "The melodrama of a hundred years ago, which was in technique and in effect a very exact theatrical counterpart of the sentimental style, can become now the romance or the medical story or detective story of television and film."[14] Or the television miniseries. In fact, the sentimental style, deployed in any century and via any form of media, is especially potent when it overlaps with the political arena, as did *Sandburg's Lincoln*.

Stephen H. Browne notes that sentimentalism, as a rhetorical style, is "inexplicable without reference to the response it is designed to evoke." "Whatever the individual expression of sentiment understood in this way, there remains one constant: as a response, sentimentalism extends no further than its own exhaustion. This exhaustion, indeed, defines precisely sentimentalism's dangerous pleasures: once consummated, it dies. Sentimentalism does not, for this reason, actually entail anything. When, therefore, the sentimental style is deployed in the service of a reform movement, its effect is apt to be paradoxical: the greater the intensity of the response, the less likely is the respondent moved to action."[15]

And what, we are right to ask, could evoke a greater emotional response than a celebratory remembrance of Lincoln's life leading up to the celebration of the nation's birth? In fairness, neither Sandburg's books nor the miniseries they inspired were part of a reform movement per se. Therefore, it would be unfair to fault *Sandburg's Lincoln* for adopting a style that discouraged its audience from doing more than merely watching. This miniseries was a text designed to entertain, not to rally, and it thus achieved its ends simply by being seen. And seen it was.

Even if *Sandburg's Lincoln* was not part of a strategic reform movement, it did perform some of the work of historical and cultural reformation even as it attached itself to a moment of national celebration. As a sentimental text, *Sandburg's Lincoln* offered a romantic vision of both Lincoln and the country. It reflected on a time that, while it might not have been simpler, appeared, at least now, to be more easily understood. The miniseries insisted that Honest Abe Lincoln was an extraordinary man, and although he had been stolen from us by the assassin's bullet, he had successfully completed his work—and our work consisted only of praising him. In 1976, the ideal citizen was a passive television viewer.

Interestingly, if *Sandburg's Lincoln* offered a respite from the political demands of the day, America's rest was short-lived—even on television. David Wolper's next major miniseries appeared on small screens all across the nation just two years later. *Roots* (1978) may be the most important made-for-television miniseries ever produced in the United States. Aimed at an audience of mostly white viewers, it recounted the horrors of American slavery in graphic detail. Not unlike Harriet Beecher Stowe's *Uncle Tom's Cabin,* which when adapted to the screen gave Lincoln his first appearance in the cinema, *Roots* demanded and received a national dialogue about race relations and civil rights in contemporary America. Functioning as something akin to an unauthorized sequel to *Sandburg's Lincoln, Roots* delivered a clear message: the occasion for celebrating America had passed, and there remained much work to be done. The time for sentiment was over, and the time for (Lincoln-like) honest self-reflection had begun. It was a new era that would, of course, call forth a new kind of Lincoln.

7

Anti-Lincoln

Gore Vidal's Lincoln (1988)

> Nothing that Sandburg ever invented was equal to Lincoln's invention of himself and, in the process, us.
>
> —Gore Vidal

> Nothing ever written about the sixteenth President was more widely read.
>
> —Merrill D. Peterson on Gore Vidal's novel *Lincoln* (1984)

The historian Don E. Fehrenbacher refers to the small but persistent movement to degrade and demean Abraham Lincoln's place in history as the "anti-Lincoln tradition."[1] Gore Vidal's controversial best seller *Lincoln* (1984) did not fall within that tradition, but it certainly resonated with it. The historical novel sparked a firestorm even before it was published, irking professional historians, angering amateur Lincoln lovers, and fascinating the American public at large. To be fair, the book does not represent Lincoln as the epitome of all evil, as did some postwar Southern depictions of the emancipator. However, Vidal's fictionalized novel presents Lincoln as a shrewd and cunning politician quite unlike the figure found in Sandburg's books or in most of Hollywood's movies. The proposition that "Abe Lincoln" was little more than a fictional construct invented by Lincoln himself and popularized by overly enthusiastic biographers is an argument that many reject but few can ignore.

Vidal's book was an enormous success. When it was announced that the novel was to be adapted into a made-for-television miniseries in 1988, the country braced itself for what was sure to be the most un-Lincoln Lincoln it had ever seen on-screen. Few were more aware than Vidal himself of the cultural consequences of such a series. After all, he had once famously suggested that America "concede the inevitable, scrap the existing educational system, and introduce the young to the past through film."[2] However, what appeared on television screens in 1988 was not an all-out attack on Lincoln, largely because it seemed not terribly interested in Lincoln.

Like the novel, which never places the reader inside Lincoln's head, the miniseries brings its audience much closer to the people around Lincoln, all of whom see Lincoln in strikingly different ways. The resulting miniseries is thus more of a meditation on perceptions and representations of Lincoln. In a way, *Gore Vidal's Lincoln* laid to rest the historical Lincoln, as if conceding finally that the man is dead and gone, and in a very postmodern move it replaced past representations with a new representation that staked little or no claim to the "real" Lincoln.

As a means of exploring this interpretation, this chapter reads *Gore Vidal's Lincoln* within two specific interpretive contexts. First, the miniseries is considered in relation to several other popular Civil War television miniseries that preceded it in the 1980s: *The Blue and the Gray* (1982), *North and South* (1985), and *North and South: Book II* (1986). None of these series was produced by the team that adapted Vidal's novel to the small screen. However, for the original audience of *Gore Vidal's Lincoln,* these other series likely sketched the larger fictionalized Civil War context in which Vidal's Abe Lincoln was situated.

Second, *Gore Vidal's Lincoln* is analyzed in relation to the so-called anti-Lincoln tradition, which has sought in various ways to change popular perceptions of America's sixteenth president. Vidal's look at Lincoln seems to have been designed not so much to assassinate Lincoln's character as to separate it from the myths that have clouded the minds of Americans—who, of course, know Lincoln only through the words of his biographers and the images of his videographers. When read in this context, the miniseries seems to reveal little about Lincoln that is proposed as true, but it discloses much about his previous representations that are supposed to be false.

Multiple Miniseries

In the early 1980s, television audiences received a crash course in Civil War history. "After years in which the Civil War remained virtually untouched as a movie or television subject," one author notes, "the 1980s suddenly presented television viewers with almost more Civil War than they could handle."[3] The sometimes highly questionable historical lessons learned in these serialized narratives very likely shaped the nation's response to the last great Civil War miniseries of the decade: *Gore Vidal's Lincoln.*

It is not entirely clear why television screens were filled with multiple miniseries about the Civil War during this era. The centennial anniversaries of the start of the war, the end of the war, and Lincoln's assassination had all come and gone in the 1960s. The country's own bicentennial had taken place in the 1970s. It is possible that the Cold War, which so completely defined the Reagan years, created a social context in which viewers were receptive to Civil War narratives, but to make that claim involves serious speculation. Whatever the reason, televised Civil War narratives flourished in the 1980s, and by the time the adaptation of Vidal's novel made it to the small screen, many viewers fancied themselves armchair experts in the history of America's only internal war.

The Blue and the Gray was the first to debut, in the fall of 1982. In it, Lincoln was but a minor player. The work concentrates on the war as witnessed by journalist and illustrator John Geyser. The narrative is very loosely based on the life of the real John Geyser, who had written for *Harper's Weekly,* fought for the Union, and kept a sketchbook during the war. In the miniseries, Geyser is a Southerner who travels to Gettysburg, Pennsylvania, to work at a newspaper. His experiences as a journalist, especially his coverage of the trial of abolitionist John Brown, lead him to conclude that slavery must be abolished.

Geyser is unable to fight for the South because of this new perspective on slavery, but he is also unwilling to fight for the North because that would mean taking up arms against his brothers, who (of course) are named Matthew, Mark, and Luke. Torn between both sides, Geyser offers a balanced perspective for his readers—and for viewers of the series. Like so many Civil War narratives, *The Blue and the Gray* represents the reality of the war by concentrating on the effect it had on two families, one Northern and one Southern, each experiencing the conflict in vastly different ways, but both at great cost.

The role of Lincoln, admittedly not central to the film, was given to legendary actor Gregory Peck. Although the Lincoln presented in this series is foremost the Savior of the Union, not the Great Emancipator, Peck was still best known for his role as Atticus Finch in the 1961 film about race relations in the South, *To Kill a Mockingbird.* By accident or design, casting Peck as Lincoln likely created a unique harmony between two Lincoln incarnations so often at odds with one another.

Still, according to one critic, Peck's performance "is one of those problematic limited portrayals . . . as you watch him, you are always aware that you are watching a famous actor dressed up like Abraham Lincoln."[4] What is most significant about the character of Lincoln in this miniseries is that he appears in all the familiar and expected places, especially at the podium. Unlike Vidal's Lincoln, played by actor Sam Waterston, who is shown making only one major speech, Peck's Lincoln delivers many, including one similar to Lincoln's speech at the train station in Springfield in 1861 and, of course, his legendary address in Gettysburg in 1863.

The Blue and the Gray thus has its Lincoln reenact well-known moments from history or, as one critic described it, Peck's Lincoln "is allowed to hit several highlights of Lincoln's time in the White House."[5] In so doing, the series provides a somewhat faithful reenactment of the historical record. Vidal's Lincoln avoids such historic scenarios almost entirely. He does not debate Douglas, he makes no speech at the Springfield train station, he does not read with great drama the words of the Emancipation Proclamation, and he recites only part of the Gettysburg Address while preparing it. If *The Blue and the Gray* is a classic example of historical reenactment, *Gore Vidal's Lincoln* is an indictment of such melodramatic re-creations.

The Blue and the Gray was followed in 1985 by *North and South,* yet another epic David L. Wolper production. Compared to *The Blue and the Gray,* this was a far more ambitious project. Both *North and South* and its sequel, *North and South: Book II,* consisted of six episodes, each ninety minutes in length. It was an epic undertaking, even by the large-scale standards of a TV miniseries. The whole endeavor was based on a popular trilogy of novels penned by the American author John Jakes. (The third novel was published in 1987, but it was not adapted to the screen until 1994 and did not include any scenes with Lincoln.) The trilogy centers on two friends and former classmates from West Point: George Hazard, a city-based Northerner whose family is in the manufacturing industry, and Orry Main, a Southerner whose family lives on a rural slave plantation. The war, of course, divides them, and their lives and experiences are symbolic of the larger national divide.

North and South is no more a Lincoln biopic than was *The Blue and the Gray.* Hal Holbrook reprises the role he played in *Sandburg's Lincoln* in the first two installments, but this time it is hardly a starring role. Because most of the action in *North and South* takes place in the 1840s and 1850s, Lincoln does not even appear until the sixth and final episode, which begins with his first inauguration and ends with the start of the war. "In *North and South,* Hal Holbrook returned to the role he had played a decade earlier. But although *North and South* was many times longer than *Sandburg's Lincoln,* Holbrook found himself much less to do. His Lincoln exists on the edges of the plot; he's there for historical purposes, not for dramatic ones."[6] Audiences apparently did not mind the lack of Lincoln, as *North and South* ranks among the most popular miniseries in television history.[7]

Although *North and South: Book II* covers Lincoln's years as president, he remained a minor character. Lincoln is on-screen much more often in *Book II* than in the earlier series, here delivering well-known speeches and worrying endlessly about the progress of the war, but the series is faithful to its focus on the Hazards of the North and the Mains of the South. This is a series of, by, and for the people—not Lincoln. He functions within the narrative to provide historical context to the personal drama on which the series concentrates.

Although Lincoln's peripheral role renders this series far less relevant than others to a project about his evolving image in movies, miniseries, and memory, its potential indirect influence is noteworthy. The size of the national audience that watched *North and South* and *North and South: Book II* was substantial, and what it witnessed was one of the most familiar and predictable depictions of Lincoln ever filmed. *North and South* and *North and South: Book II* set up those same 1980s television viewers to be surprised and in some ways alarmed by the Lincoln they were about to meet in *Gore Vidal's Lincoln.* The two portrayals could not be more different, and their proximity in time and contrast in character make compelling the argument that one could have greatly influenced the audiences' experience of the other.

The Anti-Lincoln Tradition

Lincoln has always had his detractors. During his presidency, after his assassination, throughout the twentieth century, and into the twenty-first, there have been voices and representations attempting to cut long Abe down to size. Don E. Fehrenbacher notes that historically there have been at least three major groups contributing to the anti-Lincoln tradition in America.[8]

First, Southern depictions of Lincoln during and after the war cast him as a cruel tyrant, eager for conflict and unwilling to compromise. Although Southern opposition to Lincoln was initially impersonal, focused on Northern political policy, the South quickly assigned personal blame to Lincoln for all that was lost during the war and all that was suffered during the difficult period of Reconstruction. "In speeches, sermons, and songs, in books, magazines, newspapers, pamphlets, and broadsides," Fehrenbacher concludes, Lincoln was portrayed "as a simpleton, a buffoon, a drunkard, a libertine, a physical coward, and a pornographic storyteller."[9]

Second, political rivals within Lincoln's party and in the opposition party alike did not give Lincoln much of a honeymoon after he assumed the presidency. Although their motives were quite different, both sides "charged the [Lincoln] administration with repressing civil liberties, with subverting the rights and powers of the states, and with transforming a war for defense of the Union into a revolutionary struggle for abolition and racial equality."[10]

Third, antislavery radicals in the North were nearly as frustrated by Lincoln as their proslavery counterparts in the South. Whereas the South saw Lincoln as a tyrant too quick to take destructive action, radical abolitionists in the North viewed him as too weak to act decisively, and too political to do what was right, especially if it threatened to be unpopular. All three groups challenged Lincoln while he was alive and continued to challenge popular perceptions of him after his death.

In movies and miniseries, which have tended to treat Lincoln with near-obsessive reverence, critical depictions of Lincoln are rare, but it has become acceptable to treat him as a comic figure. Attacking Abe seems not to be regarded as the stuff of popular entertainment, but taking liberties with some of the details of his life has been common practice, and in recent years Lincoln has been used as a kind of comic prop in everything from product advertisements to entertainment programming.[11] Indeed, comic depictions are about as close as Hollywood comes to anything like what Fehrenbacher calls the "anti-Lincoln tradition."

Reflections of the Past

"History is a long, long time," Edwin Black reminds us. "Its raw material is an awesome garbage heap of facts, and even the man who aspires to be nothing more than a chronicler still must make decisions about perspective."[12] That Vidal's novel never places the reader in Lincoln's head, instead presenting him only from the perspective of other characters, distances readers from his subject. His is not a book about Lincoln so much as it is a book about perceptions and representations of Lincoln, including and perhaps especially film representations.

Kenneth Burke was not referring specifically to the Hollywood biopics, although he might as well have been, when he wrote: "Even if a given terminology is a *reflection* of reality, by its very nature as a terminology it must be a *selection* of reality; and to this extent it must function also as a *deflection* of reality."[13] From this perspective, all historical "reproductions" are more accurately "representations." One cannot experience a war, for instance, any more realistically in a library than in a theater. Only symbolic representations can be experienced. Given this, I submit that the concept of hyperreality offers us a lens through which to view, and a perspective from which we may understand, Vidal's unique construction of Lincoln.

In chapter 2, I defined *hyperreality* as that which "signifies a rupture in the notion of the real brought on by techniques of mass reproduction."[14] The hyperreal is encountered whenever the fake is presented as equally good as, if not better than, the real. The Lincoln depicted in D. W. Griffith's

The Birth of a Nation established several precedents that nearly all later Lincoln films would follow, including Lincoln's appearance, his treatment by the camera and by other characters and, most notably, the most common scenarios in which he would be featured. Perhaps most influential of all was Griffith's decision, in both *The Birth of a Nation* and *Abraham Lincoln,* to eschew Lincoln's image as the Great Emancipator.

The result, I argued in chapter 2, was that nearly all subsequent Lincolns in the cinema were examples of what Umberto Eco has called the *absolute fake:* "a form of hyperreality in which a cultural artifact is perceived as an improved copy, more 'real' than its original."[15] Unlike the historical Lincoln, Griffith's character was a one-dimensional construct: universally good and fully committed to saving the Union (even if he was not terribly invested in giving freedom to slaves). This one-dimensional caricature was easily replicated by other filmmakers and digested by other audiences, far more easily than would have been the case with a more accurate and complex representation of Lincoln and his conflicting ideals.

Not so with *Gore Vidal's Lincoln.* This character is a far better example of what Jean Baudrillard has called a *simulacrum:* a representation not of the real but of other, earlier representations, with no apparent connection to anything original or authentic.[16] Like the image in a house of mirrors, Vidal's Lincoln purports to reflect nothing of the historical figure, and in fact seems to challenge the very notion that such a thing is achievable. Instead, this Lincoln reflects only other images of Lincoln, and in so doing reveals that none is any more authentic than his. Few Americans have undergone such extensive mythical abstraction as Lincoln, which highlights the increasing disparity between Lincoln (the real) and "Lincoln" (the hyperreal). As a result, as Lincoln was resurrected repeatedly in the cinema, the American people were removed ever further from him. According to this logic, Lincoln slowly descended into a perfect example of Kenneth Burke's famous phrase "rotten with perfection."[17]

Vidal's Lincoln

Gore Vidal's Lincoln aired on television in two parts, on March 27 and March 28, 1988. The series begins with what looks like Lincoln's famous train trip from the Midwest to Washington, D.C., for his inauguration. If the scene is familiar, the character is not. Lincoln arrives in disguise, and we learn that he has snuck into the city under cover of darkness amid threats of assassination. Played by actor Sam Waterston, this Lincoln is all wrong: his hat is not the usual stovepipe style, his hair beneath it is wild and untamed, and although he displays some of the folksy charm usually associated with Lincoln, it is clear from the first scene that this Lincoln's unsophisticated mannerisms and expressions are part of the disguise, designed to trick opponents into underestimating him.

The point is driven home, just minutes into the series, when one of his advisors informs Lincoln's new secretary of state, William H. Seward, that what he thought he knew about the new president was in fact "all made up for the campaign." In many respects, this is the whole project of *Gore Vidal's Lincoln:* exposing representations of Lincoln as artificial, and then replacing them with other representations, themselves likely to be equally artificial. The effect this process has on the viewer is to deliver the clear sense that we cannot and will not ever know the "real" Lincoln. He invented himself when he was alive, the series tells us, and he has been endlessly reinvented since his death.

That said, the series does make at least one clear choice: this is an exploration of a war president, a commander in chief. Other dimensions of Lincoln's life and career are mentioned in the series, most notably his troubled marriage to Mary Todd, but it is the war upon which the narrative concentrates from beginning to end. Mrs. Lincoln announces almost immediately that her husband is not an abolitionist. Rather, she insists, Lincoln wants only to prevent the spread of slavery into the new territories. Although the scene in which Mary makes this declaration serves primarily to demonstrate how difficult she is going to be as First Lady, it also functions to undercut yet another commonly held belief about the mythological Lincoln.

Indeed, most of the action that occurs before the start of the war fulfills this same purpose: to surprise the viewer with an unexpected portrayal of Lincoln, his family, his actions, and his moral commitments. For example, his son Robert is shown drinking excessively in a D.C. bar, and later searching for a brothel with John Hay. When Lincoln meets with his Cabinet, it is in a smoke-filled room that suggests an environment of political corruption not often associated with Honest Abe. Although Lincoln and Mary are rarely together and are usually fighting when they are, they still affectionately call one another "Mother" and "Father." The only constants amid all of this are the ever-present threats of an assassination and a war.

After establishing that this is not going to be the usual Lincoln biopic, the series leaps forward to April 12, 1861, and the attack on Fort Sumter that started the Civil War. Shortly afterward, Lincoln meets with his old nemesis Stephen A, Douglas to discuss the emerging battle. In a fascinating exchange, Douglas actually suggests that Lincoln free the slaves not as a matter of morality or even as a military strategy, but rather as a means of attaining fame. All of this seems distant and impersonal to Lincoln until his close friend Elmer Ellsworth is killed while removing a Confederate flag across the river in Alexandria, Virginia. If the history books record that the war began with the attack on Fort Sumter, *Gore Vidal's Lincoln* reports that Lincoln's war began with the death of his dear friend.

It is at this point that Lincoln puts General George McClellan in charge of the Union forces, a decision he will come to regret. However, if Lincoln can no longer ignore the reality of the war as it is unfolding around him, the First Lady can do so with ease. Mrs. Lincoln spends money without restraint, pushing the Lincolns deep into debt. She even resorts to leaking a copy of Lincoln's State of the Union speech to the press for a small fee. At one point, William Herndon speculates that Lincoln married Mary Todd only for political expediency. The series never endorses this theory, but its mention in the narrative keeps the focus on the tenuous relationship between what is real and what is illusion. It is as if this dichotomy exists in nearly every character and event in the series, as if to remind the audience that it too must separate fact from fiction—or at least one fiction from another.

After the sudden and tragic death of their son Willie, both his parents are distraught. Although each attempts to grieve in isolation, healing begins only after they reunite. The Lincolns' personal tragedy, their temporary division, and their eventual reunification foreshadow the war and its aftermath in obvious ways. Following this segment, the series moves forward to Lincoln's signing of the Emancipation Proclamation. The event is depicted in a most unusual manner. Foremost, it is abundantly clear from Lincoln and other characters that this is a strategic move prompted by military and not moral concerns. It is emphasized repeatedly that Lincoln has decided to free the slaves only in Southern states that are in rebellion.

In addition, the series moves immediately from this to one of the most remarkable and unsettling scenes in the whole history of Lincoln films. Meeting with a group of African American men in the White House, Lincoln proposes that "Negroes" be given land in Central America. Lincoln tells the men: "It is better for us both to be separated." When they refuse to accept his offer, Lincoln concedes that his upbringing in the Midwest probably made him biased on the question of racial equality. Although the series gives Lincoln credit for recognizing this, it casually attributes such regional racism to him nonetheless.

After weathering a difficult midterm election in 1862 in which the Republicans manage to maintain control of Congress, Lincoln finally feels emboldened to replace General McClellan. Throughout this difficult period, the series continues to emphasize that many of Lincoln's best-known characteristics were in fact carefully rehearsed affectations designed to help him in the political arena. For example, of his penchant for storytelling, Lincoln states: "When there is so much you cannot say, it's always a good idea to have a story ready." His son Robert reinforces the point, noting that his father "hates his past, all this rail-splitter stuff." The series also provides a few glimpses of Lincoln that are quite uncharacteristic. After the Union suffers a defeat at Fredericksburg, for example, Lincoln loses his composure, yells at his staff, and announces that he has had enough of this war.

After finally placing General Grant in charge of the Union army, Lincoln must prepare for his own experience at Gettysburg. Interestingly, the series permits the audience to see Lincoln as he composes his famous speech, but not as he delivers it. Instead of watching him give his legendary speech before a large crowd at the battle site, we see him in small room in a train station still crafting his remarks and wondering what the keynote speaker of the day, Edward Everett, will say. "You know," Lincoln tells his companions, "I have heard of Everett all my life and he has always been famous, but I never could find out why. . . . There are people like that in public life." It is a small moment in the narrative, but one that seems to represent the work of the series as a whole.

Having won the nomination against Salmon P. Chase and then the 1864 election—a victory that Lincoln admits was secured by much wheeling and dealing—Lincoln receives news of the victory that means the most to him. Grant has finally won the war. Here the series breaks with its own tradition of avoiding Lincoln's most familiar public moments when it re-creates the delivery of his famous and eloquent second inaugural address. The scene is in no way remarkable except for the fact that it presents a fairly faithful re-creation of the audience's collective understanding of the speech. Rather than challenging what the audience thought it knew, the series here presents Lincoln's reelection just as the audience has expected, with measured joy and grand eloquence.

Yet while the North celebrates dual victories of ballots and bullets, Lincoln is surrounded by would-be assassins. In a scene that is most unusual in the whole history of Lincoln films, Lincoln dreams of his own death. Other movies reference this moment; this one dramatizes it. Like Dickens's Scrooge, Lincoln wanders about in a state somewhere between life and death. He sees himself lying in state in the White House, and he is clearly terrified by the vision. Lincoln awakens from the nightmare shaken. From a dramatic point of view, it is an interesting choice to film the actual dream. Of course, the audience knows what is soon to befall Lincoln, but our expectation is that he does not know. This dramatic irony is eliminated by the dream, which appears to give this Lincoln a clear knowledge of his fate. After a long series in which the audience felt quite alienated from this unusual Lincoln, the nightmare unites the character and the audience in their shared knowledge of the tragedy to come.

On April 14, 1865, Lincoln enjoys a carriage ride to the theater with his wife and seems entirely at peace. The assassination scene in *Gore Vidal's Lincoln* is presented in great detail, unlike most Lincoln films. The audience is spared a representation of the actual moment of the attack, but the setup and aftermath are far more detailed than is shown in any other major film or miniseries. After Booth makes his way into the president's box and commits his crime, Lincoln's body is hurried across the street to a boardinghouse. Mary is hysterical; before being removed from the room, she blames Lincoln for not letting the South leave the Union.

After Lincoln's death, the series ends just as it began—with a train ride across the country. This time, of course, Lincoln is headed home, to Illinois, where the story of his life also began and now ends. The crowds of citizens shown awaiting the train as it slowly moves across the reunited nation provide assurance that even Vidal's Lincoln will earn his rightful place in history, remembered for his victories, even if they were won with greater cunning and calculation than the history books are willing to acknowledge. In voice-over, we hear Lincoln say, "We cannot escape history. We will be remembered in spite of ourselves."

Gore Vidal's Lincoln may be best understood placed within two interpretive contexts. First, several other popular Civil War miniseries aired in the years immediately before the broadcast of *Gore Vidal's Lincoln. The Blue and the Gray, North and South,* and *North and South: Book II* enjoyed large television audiences and thus likely contributed to the information (or misinformation) about Lincoln and the war upon which audiences drew in order to make sense of Vidal's unorthodox presentation of Abe Lincoln. Second, *Gore Vidal's Lincoln* resonates in interesting ways with the so-called anti-Lincoln tradition. This tradition has challenged popular perceptions of Lincoln by recasting him as a villain in revisionist Civil War narratives.

The figure of Lincoln in this miniseries differs significantly from the depictions of Lincoln found in nearly every other major film or miniseries. However, rather than recast Lincoln as a villain, as some feared Vidal was determined to do, this representation complicated the simplistic two-dimensionality of other representations. The miniseries goes to great lengths to demonstrate that what passes for popular knowledge about Lincoln is largely fiction—invented either by the man himself or by his biographers.

The concept of hyperreality illuminates the ways in which Vidal's representation of Lincoln was defined in relation to preexisting representations of Lincoln. One might conclude that the miniseries, as a simulation of previous simulations, implies that the "real" Lincoln is gone forever.

However, the series does not make this point in any explicit way. True, it is clear to even the casual viewer that Sam Waterson's portrayal of Lincoln is very different from the norm, but the series does not concede that its representation is just that—a representation. Thus it is possible that viewers of this series may have come away thinking that they had finally gotten some sense of what the "real" Lincoln was like. If this was the case, it is unfortunate. In the cinema, we cannot find the "real" Lincoln, only the "reel" Lincoln.

Notes

Introduction

1. Merrill D. Peterson, *Lincoln in American Memory* (New York: Oxford University Press, 1994), 4.

2. Don E. Fehrenbacher, *Lincoln in Text and Context: Collected Essays* (Stanford, Calif.: Stanford University Press, 1987), 181–82.

3. David H. Donald, *Lincoln Reconsidered: Essays on the Civil War Era* (New York: Knopf, 1966), 145.

4. Harold Holzer, Gabor S. Boritt, and Mark E. Neely Jr., *Changing the Lincoln Image* (Fort Wayne, Ind.: Louis A. Warren Lincoln Library and Museum, 1985), 149.

5. Peterson, *Lincoln in American Memory,* 4.

6. Barry Schwartz, *Abraham Lincoln and the Forge of National Memory* (Chicago: University of Chicago Press, 2000), 84.

7. Ibid., 110–11.

8. Peterson, *Lincoln in American Memory,* 175.

9. Schwartz, *Abraham Lincoln,* 301.

10. Peterson, *Lincoln in American Memory,* 175–76.

11. Schwartz, *Abraham Lincoln,* 284–85.

12. Ibid., 286.

13. Ibid., 290.

14. Donald, *Lincoln Reconsidered,* 148–49.

15. Waldo W. Braden, ed., *Building the Myth: Selected Speeches Memorializing Abraham Lincoln* (Urbana: University of Illinois Press, 1990), 191–92.

16. Scott A. Sandage, "A Marble House Divided: The Lincoln Memorial, the Civil Rights Movement, and the Politics of Memory, 1939–1963," *Journal of American History* 80 (June 1993): 143.

17. Peterson, *Lincoln in American Memory,* 362–63.

18. Harold Holzer, ed., *The Lincoln-Douglas Debates* (New York: HarperPerennial, 1993), 63.

19. Fehrenbacher, *Lincoln in Text and Context,* 197–213.

20. Schwartz, *Abraham Lincoln,* 5.

21. Sandage, "Marble House," 141.

22. Garry Wills, *Lincoln at Gettysburg: The Words That Remade America* (New York: Simon & Schuster, 1992).

23. Ibid., 38.

24. Maurice Halbwachs, *On Collective Memory,* trans. Lewis A. Cosner (Chicago: University of Chicago Press, 1992), 40.

25. John Bodnar, *Remaking America: Public Memory, Commemoration, and Patriotism in the Twentieth Century* (Princeton, N.J.: Princeton University Press, 1992), 15.

26. Michael Kammen, *Mystic Chords of Memory: The Transformation of Tradition in American Culture* (New York: Knopf, 1991), 13.

27. Gary R. Edgerton, "Introduction: Television as Historian; A Different Kind of History Altogether," in *Television Histories: Shaping Collective Memory in the Media Age,* ed. Gary R. Edgerton and Peter C. Rollins (Lexington: University Press of Kentucky, 2001), 5.

28. An excellent summary of such work is in Carole Blair, Greg Dickinson, and Brian L. Ott, "Introduction: Rhetoric/Memory/Place," in *Places of Public Memory: The Rhetoric of Museums and Memorials,* ed. Greg Dickinson, Carole Blair, and Brian L. Ott (Tuscaloosa: University of Alabama Press, 2010), 1-54.

29. Kendall R. Phillips, introduction to *Framing Public Memory,* ed. Kendall R. Phillips (Tuscaloosa: University of Alabama Press, 2004), 3.

30. Blair, Dickinson, and Ott, "Introduction: Rhetoric/Memory/Place," 6.

31. Alison Landsberg, *Prosthetic Memory: The Transformation of American Remembrance in the Age of Mass Culture* (New York: Columbia University Press, 2004), 11, 3.

32. Barbie Zelizer, "The Voice of the Visual in Memory," in Phillips, *Framing Public Memory,* 158.

33. Landsberg, *Prosthetic Memory,* 14.

34. See, for example, John E. O'Connor, Martin A. Jackson, and Arthur M. Schlesinger Jr., eds., *American History / American Film: Interpreting the Hollywood Image* (New York: Ungar, 1988); Peter C. Rollins and John E. O'Connor, eds., *Hollywood's West: The American Frontier in Film, Television, and History* (Lexington: University Press of Kentucky, 2009); Peter C. Rollins and John E. O'Connor, eds., *The West Wing: The American Presidency as Television Drama* (Syracuse, N.Y.: Syracuse University Press, 2003); John E. O'Connor, *Image as Artifact: The Historical Analysis of Film and Television* (Malabar, Fla.: Robert E. Krieger, 1990); Peter C. Rollins and John E. O'Connor, eds., *Why We Fought: America's Wars in Film and History* (Lexington: University Press of Kentucky, 2008); Peter C. Rollins and John E. O'Connor, eds., *Hollywood's White House: The American Presidency in Film and History* (Lexington: University Press of Kentucky, 2005); Peter C. Rollins and John E. O'Connor, eds., *Hollywood's Indian: The Portrayal of the Native American in Film* (Lexington: University Press of Kentucky, 2003); Peter C. Rollins, *Hollywood as Historian: American Film in a Cultural Context* (Lexington: University Press of Kentucky, 1997); Peter C. Rollins, ed., *The Columbia Companion to American History on Film: How the Movies Have Portrayed the American Past* (New York: Columbia University Press, 2006);

Robert Brent Toplin, *Oliver Stone's USA: Film, History and Controversy* (Lawrence: University Press of Kansas, 2003); Robert Brent Toplin, *Reel History* (Lawrence: University Press of Kansas, 2002); Robert Brent Toplin, ed., *Ken Burns'* The Civil War: *Historians Respond* (New York: Oxford University Press, 1997); Robert Brent Toplin, *History by Hollywood: The Use and Abuse of the American Past* (Champaign: University of Illinois Press, 1996).

35. Paul Grainge, ed., *Memory and Popular Film* (Manchester: Manchester University Press), 1.

36. Foucault, "Film and Popular Memory," 123.

37. Peterson, *Lincoln in American Memory;* Schwartz, *Abraham Lincoln;* Barry Schwartz, *Abraham Lincoln in the Post-heroic Era: History and Memory in Late Twentieth-Century America* (Chicago: University of Chicago Press, 2009); Fehrenbacher, *Lincoln in Text and Context;* Harold Holzer, Gabor S. Boritt, and Mark E. Neely, *The Lincoln Image: Abraham Lincoln and the Popular Print* (Champagne: University of Illinois Press, 2005); Philip B. Kunhardt III, Peter W. Kunhardt, and Peter W. Kunhardt Jr., *Looking for Lincoln: The Making of an American Icon* (New York: Knopf, 2011); Edward Steers Jr., *Lincoln Legends: Myths, Hoaxes, and Confabulations Associated with Our Greatest President* (Lexington: University Press of Kentucky, 2009).

38. See, for example, Frank Thompson, *Abraham Lincoln: Twentieth-Century Popular Portrayals* (Dallas: Taylor Trade, 1999); or Bruce Chadwick, *The Reel Civil War: Mythmaking in American Film* (New York: Vintage Books, 2002).

39. See, for example, Michael G. Krukones, "Motion Picture Presidents of the 1930s: Factual and Fictional Leaders for a Time of Crisis," in Rollins and O'Connor, *Hollywood's White House,* 143–58; Robert C. Roman, "Lincoln on the Screen," *Films in Review* 2 (1961): 87–101.

40. Doris Kearns Goodwin, *Team of Rivals: The Political Genius of Abraham Lincoln* (New York: Simon & Schuster, 2005). See C. A. Tripp, *The Intimate World of Abraham Lincoln* (New York: Basic Books, 2006).

1. Great Emancipator: Lincoln before Lincoln *(2012)*

1. See Doris Kearns Goodwin, *Team of Rivals: The Political Genius of Abraham Lincoln* (New York: Simon & Schuster, 2005); Seth Grahame-Smith, *Abraham Lincoln: Vampire Hunter* (New York: Grand Central, 2010).

2. Barry Schwartz, "Iconography and Collective Memory: Lincoln's Image in the American Mind," *Sociological Quarterly* 32 (Autumn 1991): 301.

3. George F. Custen, *Bio/Pics: How Hollywood Constructed Public History* (New Brunswick, N.J.: Rutgers University Press, 1992).

4. See Mark S. Reinhart, *Abraham Lincoln on Screen: A Filmography of Dramas and Documentaries, Including Television, 1903–1998* (Jefferson, N.C.: McFarland, 1999). Reinhart has gathered what is undoubtedly the definitive list of Abraham Lincoln appearances in film and television. Although the book offers

little by way of in-depth analysis, it offers production details and plot summaries of hundreds of movies, miniseries, and television series and specials. It is an invaluable guide, one without which writing this book might not have been possible.

5. Ibid., 137.

6. For an analysis of the Armstrong case, see John Evangelist Walsh, *Moonlight: Abraham Lincoln and the Almanac Trial* (New York: St. Martin's, 2000).

7. Reinhart, *Abraham Lincoln,* 89.

8. Ibid., 91.

9. Ibid., 108.

10. Ibid., 207.

11. Ibid., 50.

12. Ibid., 163.

13. Michael Fleming, "Lincoln Logs in at Dream Works," *Variety,* January 11, 2005, http://variety.com/2005/film/news/lincoln-logs-in-at-dreamworks-1117916168/ (accessed January 5, 2015).

2. Great Heart: The Birth of a Nation *(1915)*

1. David Bordwell, Janet Staiger, and Kristin Thompson, *The Classical Hollywood Cinema: Film Style and Mode of Production to 1960* (New York: Columbia University Press, 1985), 157.

2. Ibid., 3.

3. Robert Brent Toplin, *History by Hollywood: The Use and Abuse of the American Past* (Urbana: University of Illinois Press, 1996), ix.

4. Jim Cullen, *The Civil War in Popular Culture: A Reusable Past* (Washington, D.C.: Smithsonian Institution Press, 1995), 13.

5. George F. Custen, *Bio/Pics: How Hollywood Constructed Public History* (New Brunswick, N.J.: Rutgers University Press, 1992), 7.

6. Robert A. Rosenstone, *Visions of the Past: The Challenge of Film to Our Idea of History* (Cambridge, Mass.: Harvard University Press, 1995), 70.

7. Ibid., 13.

8. Warren Goldstein, "Bad History Is Bad for a Culture," *Chronicle of Higher Education,* April 1998, A64.

9. Clyde Taylor, "The Rebirth of the Aesthetic in Cinema," in *The Birth of Whiteness: Race and the Emergence of U.S. Cinema,* ed. Daniel Bernardi (New Brunswick, N.J.: Rutgers University Press, 1996), 15.

10. Of the many book-length treatments of this film, perhaps the best is Melvyn Stokes's *DW Griffith's "The Birth of a Nation": A History of "the Most Controversial Motion Picture of All Time"* (New York: Oxford University Press, 2007).

11. Michael R. Hurwitz, *DW Griffith's "The Birth of a Nation": The Film That Transformed America* (N.p.: BookSurge, 2006), xi.

12. Jon Lewis, *American Film: A History* (New York: Norton, 2008), 32.

13. Ibid.

14. Although *Abraham Lincoln* was received poorly by both audiences and critics, it has since come to be regarded as one of the most important and influential of all Lincoln films. It is examined in detail in chapter 3.

15. The title of this ten-volume biography, published in 1890, is *Abraham Lincoln: A History*. Written by two of Lincoln's secretaries, it is at once a firsthand account but also obviously biased.

16. Mark S. Reinhart, *Abraham Lincoln on Screen: A Filmography of Dramas and Documentaries, Including Television, 1903–1998* (Jefferson, N.C.: McFarland, 1999), 88.

17. See, for example: Stokes, *DW Griffith's "The Birth of a Nation,"* 188; or Robert Lang, "*The Birth of a Nation:* History, Ideology, Narrative Form," in *"The Birth of a Nation": DW Griffith, Director*, ed. Robert Lang (New Brunswick, N.J.: Rutgers University Press, 1994), 23.

18. Reinhart, *Abraham Lincoln on Screen*, 73.

19. Stokes, *DW Griffith's "The Birth of a Nation,"* 189.

20. Ibid., 116.

21. Steven Best and Douglas Kellner, "Debord and the Postmodern Turn: New Stages of the Spectacle," *Illuminations*, n.d., http://csmt.uchicago.edu/glossary2004/realityhyperreality.htm (accessed April 1, 2009).

22. Jaap Kooijman, *Fabricating the Absolute Fake: "America" in Contemporary Pop Culture* (Amsterdam: Amsterdam University Press, 2008), 17.

23. Jean Baudrillard, "Simulations and Simularca," in *Selected Writings*, 2nd ed., ed. Mark Poster (Cambridge: Blackwell, 2002), 180.

24. Umberto Eco, *Travels in Hyperreality*, trans. William Weaver (New York: Harcourt Brace, 1983), 8.

25. Garry Wills, *Lincoln at Gettysburg: The Words That Remade America* (New York: Simon & Schuster, 1992), 38.

3. Savior of the Union: Abraham Lincoln *(1930)*

1. Stephen Vincent Benét, *Selected Letters of Stephen Vincent Benét*, ed. Charles A. Fenton (New Haven: Yale University Press, 1960), 201.

2. Lary May, *Screening out the Past: The Birth of Mass Culture and the Motion Picture Industry* (New York: Oxford University Press, 1980), 61.

3. James Hart, ed., *The Man Who Invented Hollywood: The Autobiography of D. W. Griffith* (Louisville: Touchstone, 1972), 23.

4. Ibid., 26.

5. Robert M. Henderson, *D. W. Griffith: His Life and Work* (New York: Oxford University Press, 1972), 274.

6. Edmund Wilson, *Letters on Literature and Politics* (New York: Farrar, Straus & Giroux, 1972), 610.

7. Richard Schickel, *D. W. Griffith: An American Life* (New York: Simon & Schuster, 1984), 551–52.

8. Ibid., 552.

9. Benét, *Selected Letters,* 234.

10. Ibid., 199.

11. Ibid., 238.

12. Michael R. Pitts, ed., *Hollywood and American History: A Filmography of over 250 Motion Pictures Depicting U.S. History* (Jefferson, N.C.: McFarland, 1994), 18.

13. Martin Williams, *Griffith: First Artist of the Movies* (New York: Oxford University Press, 1980), 150.

14. Ibid., 151.

15. Henderson, *D.W. Griffith,* 273.

16. Schickel, *D.W. Griffith,* 553–54.

17. Benét, *Selected Letters,* 195.

18. Ibid., 201.

19. Henderson, *D.W. Griffith,* 274.

20. *Variety Film Reviews: 1907–1980* (New York: Garland, 1983), 1.

21. Schickel, *D.W. Griffith,* 557.

22. Merrill D. Peterson, *Lincoln in American Memory* (New York: Oxford University Press, 1994), 344.

23. Henderson, *D.W. Griffith,* 274–75.

24. Schickel, *D.W. Griffith,* 557.

25. Andrew Sarris, "David Lewelyn Wark Griffith," in *Encyclopedia of American Biography,* 2nd ed., ed. John A. Garraty and Jerome L. Sternstein (New York: HarperCollins, 1996), 477.

26. Peterson, *Lincoln in American Memory,* 345.

27. Don E. Fehrenbacher, *Lincoln in Text and Context* (Stanford, Calif.: Stanford University Press, 1987), 231.

28. David Herbert Donald, *Lincoln Reconsidered: Essays on the Civil War Era,* 2nd ed. (New York: Knopf, 1966), 148–49.

29. George F. Custen, *Bio/Pics: How Hollywood Constructed Public History* (New Brunswick, N.J.: Rutgers University Press, 1992), 150.

30. Ibid., 151.

31. Ibid., 154.

32. Similar versions of this line are delivered in three films analyzed in this book. In *Young Mr. Lincoln,* a character named Big Buck tells Henry Fonda's Lincoln, "I'm the biggest buck in this lick." And in *Abe Lincoln in Illinois,* it is Jack Armstrong who tells Raymond Massey's Lincoln, "I'm the big buck in this lick."

33. Custen, *Bio/Pics,* 164–65.

34. See David Zarefsky, *Lincoln, Douglas, and Slavery: In the Crucible of Public Debate* (Chicago: University of Chicago Press, 1993).

35. Waldo W. Braden, *Abraham Lincoln: Public Speaker* (Baton Rouge: Louisiana State University Press, 1988), 81, 83, 43.

36. Jay Robert Nash and Stanley Ralph Ross, *The Motion Picture Guide: 1927-1984* (Chicago: Cinebooks, 1985), 5.

4. *Great Commoner:* Young Mr. Lincoln *(1939)*

1. This sobriquet, of course, is often used to refer to William Jennings Bryan. Its application to Lincoln in *Young Mr. Lincoln* is part of what makes the film so interesting.

2. Sergei Eisenstein, "A Dialectical Approach to Film Form," in *Film Form: Essays in Film Theory* (New York: Harcourt, 1969), 46.

3. Naveh Eyal, "'He Belongs to the Ages': Lincoln's Image and the American Historical Consciousness," *Journal of American Culture* 16 (Winter 1993): 50.

4. Ben Brewster, "Notes on the Text 'John Ford's *Young Mr. Lincoln*' by the Editors of *Cahiers du Cinéma*," *Screen* 13 (1973): 40.

5. Barry Schwartz, "Iconography and Collective Memory: Lincoln's Image in the American Mind," *Sociological Quarterly* 32 (1991): 301–2.

6. Merrill D. Peterson, *Lincoln in American Memory* (New York: Oxford University Press, 1994), 176.

7. Jennifer Lawn, "Four Characters in Search of a Narrator: Focalization and the Representation of Consciousness in *Under the Volcano*," *Studies in Canadian Literature* 18 (1993), https://journals.lib.unb.ca/index.php/SCL/article/view/8187/9244 (accessed November 9, 2009).

8. David Bordwell, *Narration in the Fiction Film* (Madison: University of Wisconsin Press, 1985), 3.

9. David A. Cook, *A History of Narrative Film*, 4th ed. (New York: Norton, 2004), 148.

10. Ibid., 155.

11. Ibid., 149.

12. Martin Williams, *Griffith: First Artist of the Movies* (New York: Oxford University Press, 1980), 151.

13. "*Young Mr. Lincoln*," *Time*, June 12, 1939, 78.

14. "John Ford's *Young Mr. Lincoln:* A Collective Text by the Editors of *Cahiers du Cinéma*," in *Movies and Methods: An Anthology*, 2nd ed., ed. Bill Nichols (Berkeley: University of California Press, 1985), 498.

15. Ibid., 499.

16. See Tag Gallagher, *John Ford: The Man and His Movies* (Berkeley: University of California Press, 1986); Andrew Sarris, *The John Ford Movie Mystery* (Bloomington: Indiana University Press, 1975); Michael Kerbel, *Henry Fonda* (New York: Pyramid, 1975).

17. See Bruce Chadwick, *The Reel Civil War: Mythmaking in American Film* (New York: Knopf, 2001), 151–82; Peterson, *Lincoln in American Memory*, 344–45; Frank Thompson, *Abraham Lincoln: Twentieth-Century Popular Portrayals* (Dallas: Taylor, 1999), 177–89.

18. See David Bordwell, *Making Meaning: Inference and Rhetoric in the Interpretation of the Cinema* (Cambridge: Harvard University Press, 1989), 84–87; Brewster, "Notes on the Text"; Nick Browne, "*Cahiers du Cinéma*'s Rereading of Hollywood Cinema: An Analysis of Method," *Quarterly Review of Film Studies* 3 (1978): 405–16; Brian Henderson, "Critique of Cine-Structuralism," *Film Quarterly* 27 (1973–1974): 37–46.

19. Browne, "An Analysis of Method," 405.

20. See Bordwell, *Making Meaning,* 84–87; Brewster, "Notes on the Text"; Browne, "An Analysis of Method"; Nick Browne, "The Spectator of American Symbolic Forms: Re-reading John Ford's *Young Mr. Lincoln,*" *Film Reader* 4 (1980): 180–88; Henderson, "Critique of Cine-Structuralism."

21. See William Darby, "Musical Links in *Young Mr. Lincoln, My Darling Clementine,* and *The Man Who Shot Liberty Valance,*" *Cinema Journal* 31 (1991): 22–36; Marsha Kinder, "The Image of Patriarchal Power in *Young Mr. Lincoln* (1939) and *Ivan the Terrible, Part I* (1945)," *Film Quarterly* 39 (1985-1986): 29–49.

22. See John Evangelist Walsh, *Moonlight: Abraham Lincoln and the Almanac Trial* (New York: St. Martin's, 2000).

23. Bordwell, *Making Meaning,* 85–86.

24. Browne, "An Analysis of Method," 406.

25. Browne, "The Spectator," 185.

26. Edwin Black, *Rhetorical Questions: Studies of Public Discourse* (Chicago: University of Chicago Press, 1992), 52.

27. Quoted in Kinder, "The Image of Patriarchal Power," 29; emphasis added.

28. For an exhaustive analysis of the music in this and other John Ford films, see Darby, "Musical Links."

29. Browne, "The Spectator," 186.

30. Kinder, "The Image of Patriarchal Power," 30.

31. "John Ford's *Young Mr. Lincoln,*" 503.

32. Ibid., 504.

33. Browne, "The Spectator," 181.

34. Ibid., 186–87.

35. Darby, "Musical Links," 25.

36. For an analysis that concentrates entirely on the film's treatment of the law, see Norman Rosenberg, "*Young Mr. Lincoln:* The Lawyer as Super-hero," *Legal Studies Forum* 15 (1991): 215–29.

37. Marouf Hasian Jr., "Jurisprudence as Performance: John Brown's Enactment of Natural Law at Harper's Ferry," *Quarterly Journal of Speech* 86 (2000): 190.

38. Browne, "The Spectator," 184–85.

39. Gallagher, *John Ford,* 163–64.

40. Brewster, "Notes on the Text," 37. *Young Tom Edison* (1940), *Young Daniel Boone* (1959), *Young Jesse James* (1960), *Young Sherlock Holmes* (1985), and *Young Einstein* (1988) are just a few of the many popular films that center on the early

life of a historical or fictional figure known to achieve fame or notoriety later in life.

41. Gallagher, *John Ford,* 162–63, 166.

42. "*Young Mr. Lincoln,*" *Magill's Survey of Cinema—English Language Films, First Series* (Englewood Cliffs, N.J.: Salem, 1980), 1900.

43. "John Ford's *Young Mr. Lincoln,*" 511.

44. Kinder, "The Image of Patriarchal Power," 33–34.

45. "John Ford's *Young Mr. Lincoln,*" 511–12.

46. Kinder, "The Image of Patriarchal Power," 34.

47. John Ford's *Young Mr. Lincoln,*" 513–14.

48. Lincoln's speech, far more eloquent than the one he delivered in the film's opening scene, is further interesting in that multiple texts resonate within it. First, some viewers will recognize that the action and the dialogue are noticeably similar to Carl Sandburg's treatment in *Abraham Lincoln: The Prairie Years* of a fistfight that allegedly took place in Lincoln's youth. Second, the scene evokes at least two different parts of the Bible: the book of Jeremiah, in which the ineloquent Jeremiah must act as a reluctant prophet, just as Lincoln does in the film, and the Sermon on the Mount, from which Lincoln quotes. Finally, the scene has been so influential in Hollywood that it has been re-created in several films, most notably in the equally famous jail scene in *To Kill a Mockingbird* (1961).

49. For works on Lincoln and silence, see Edwin Black, "Gettysburg and Silence," *Quarterly Journal of Speech* 80 (1994): 21–36; Waldo Braden, *Abraham Lincoln, Public Speaker* (Baton Rouge: Louisiana State University Press, 1988), 37–47; Robert G. Gunderson, "Lincoln and the Policy of Eloquent Silence," *Quarterly Journal of Speech* 47 (1961): 1–9; Jeffrey Tulis, *The Rhetorical Presidency* (Princeton, N.J.: Princeton University Press, 1987), 79–81.

50. Browne, "The Spectator," 184.

5. *First American:* Abe Lincoln in Illinois *(1940)*

1. Merrill D. Peterson, *Lincoln in American Memory* (New York: Oxford University Press, 1994), 345.

2. Robert E. Sherwood, *Abe Lincoln in Illinois: A Play in Twelve Scenes,* 2nd ed. (New York: Charles Scribner's Sons, 1939), 189.

3. Raymond Massey, *A Hundred Different Lives* (Boston: Little, Brown, 1979), 230.

4. Ibid., 232.

5. Ibid., 245.

6. Ibid., 247.

7. Ibid., 248.

8. Ibid., 230.

9. Sherwood, *Abe Lincoln in Illinois,* 121–22.

10. Massey, *A Hundred Different Lives,* 230, 253.

11. John Mason Brown, *The Ordeal of a Playwright: Robert E. Sherwood and the Challenge of War* (New York: Harper & Row, 1970), 77–78.

12. Massey, *A Hundred Different Lives,* 254.

13. Roland Barthes, *Image-Music Text,* trans. Stephen Heath (New York: Hill & Wang, 1977), 145, 146–48.

14. David Bordwell, *Narration in the Fiction Film* (Madison: University of Wisconsin Press, 1985), 7.

15. Kristin Thompson, "The Concept of Cinematic Excess," in *Narrative, Apparatus, Ideology: A Film Theory Reader,* ed. Philip Rosen (New York: Columbia University Press, 1986), 141.

16. Lea Jacobs and Richard de Cordova, "Spectacle and Narrative Theory," *Quarterly Review of Film Studies* 7 (Fall 1982): 294.

17. Bordwell, *Narration in the Fiction Film,* 49–50, 52.

18. Robert A. Rosenstone, *Visions of the Past: The Challenge of Film to Our Idea of History* (Cambridge, Mass.: Harvard University Press, 1995), 123.

19. Frank S. Nugent, "Abe Lincoln in Illinois," *New York Times,* February 23, 1940, 19.

20. R. Baird Shuman, *Robert E. Sherwood* (New York: Twayne, 1964), 84–85.

21. Peterson, *Lincoln in American Memory,* 386.

22. Harold Holzer, ed., *The Lincoln-Douglas Debates* (New York: HarperPerennial, 1993), ix.

23. Sherwood, *Abe Lincoln in Illinois,* 203.

24. Thomas W. Benson and Carolyn Anderson, "The Ultimate Technology: Frederick Wiseman's *Missile,*" in *Communication and the Culture of Technology,* ed. Martin J. Medhurst, Alberto Gonzalez, and Tarla Rai Peterson (Pullman: Washington State University Press, 1990), 259.

25. Sherwood, *Abe Lincoln in Illinois,* 220.

26. Bruce F. Kawin, *Mindscreen: Bergman, Godard, and First-Person Film* (Princeton, N.J.: Princeton University Press, 1978), 10.

27. Sherwood, *Abe Lincoln in Illinois,* 223.

28. Ibid., 231.

29. Ibid., 246.

6. *Honest Abe:* Sandburg's Lincoln *(1974–1976)*

1. Mark S. Reinhart, *Abraham Lincoln on the Screen: A Filmography of Dramas and Documentaries, Including Television, 1903–1998* (Jefferson, N.C.: McFarland, 1999), 53, 51.

2. Ibid., 53.

3. Ibid.

4. James Hurt, "Sandburg's *Lincoln* within History," *Journal of the Abraham Lincoln Association* 20 (Winter 1999): 55.

5. Reinhart, *Abraham Lincoln on the Screen,* 232.

6. See Jason Emerson, *The Madness of Mary Lincoln* (Carbondale: Southern Illinois University Press, 2007).

7. Frank Thompson, *Abraham Lincoln: Twentieth-Century Popular Portrayals* (Dallas: Taylor, 1999), 80.

8. Ibid., 83.

9. Hugh McCulloch, *Men and Measures of a Half a Century* (Whitefish, Mont.: Kessinger, 2008), 188.

10. Reinhart, *Abraham Lincoln on the Screen,* 232.

11. "Abraham Lincoln to Eliza Caldwell (Mrs. Orville H.) Browning, 1 April 1838," in *The Collected Works of Abraham Lincoln,* ed. Roy P. Basler (New Brunswick, N.J.: Rutgers University Press), 1:118.

12. Reinhart, *Abraham Lincoln on the Screen,* 233.

13. For the conflation of Lincoln and the civil rights movement, see, for example, Scott A. Sandage, "A Marble House Divided: The Lincoln Memorial, the Civil Rights Movement, and the Politics of Memory, 1939–1963," *Journal of American History* 80 (June 1993): 135–67.

14. Black, "The Sentimental Style as Escapism," 99, 111.

15. Stephen H. Browne, "'Like Gory Spectres': Representing Evil in Theodore Weld's *American Slavery as It Is,*" *Quarterly Journal of Speech* 80 (August 1994): 278.

7. *Anti-Lincoln:* Gore Vidal's Lincoln *(1988)*

1. Don E. Fehrenbacher, *Lincoln in Text and Context: Collected Essays* (Stanford, Calif.: Stanford University Press, 1987), 197–213.

2. Mark C. Carnes, *Past Imperfect: History according to the Movies* (New York: Henry Holt, 1996), 9.

3. Frank Thompson, *Abraham Lincoln: Twentieth-Century Popular Portrayals* (Dallas: Taylor, 1999), 89.

4. Mark S. Reinhart, *Abraham Lincoln on Screen: A Filmography of Dramas and Documentaries, Including Television, 1903–1998* (Jefferson, N.C.: McFarland, 1999), 79.

5. Thompson, *Abraham Lincoln,* 95.

6. Ibid., 90.

7. Mark Bennett, "John Jakes' Journey to *New York Times* Bestseller List Included Boyhood Years in Terre Haute," *Tribune-Star,* August 11, 2007, http://tribstar.com/features/x1155705071/John-Jakes-journey-to-New-York-Times-bestseller-list-included-boyhood-years-in-Terre-Haute (accessed April 26, 2011).

8. Fehrenbacher, *Lincoln in Text and Context,* 198.

9. Ibid., 199.

10. Ibid., 199–200.

11. See Jackie Hogan, *Lincoln, Inc.: Selling the Sixteenth President in Contemporary America* (New York: Rowman & Littlefield, 2011).

12. Edwin Black, "The Second Persona," in *Landmark Essays in Rhetorical Criticism,* ed. Thomas W. Benson (Mahwah, N.J.: Hermagoras, 1993), 161.

13. Kenneth Burke, *Language as Symbolic Action: Essays on Life, Literature, and Method* (Berkeley: University of California Press, 1966), 45.

14. Steven Best and Douglas Kellner, "Debord and the Postmodern Turn: New Stages of the Spectacle," *Illuminations,* n.d., http://csmt.uchicago.edu/glossary2004/realityhyperreality.htm (accessed April 1, 2009).

15. Jaap Kooijman, *Fabricating the Absolute Fake: America in Contemporary Pop Culture* (Amsterdam: Amsterdam University Press, 2008), 10.

16. Jean Baudrillard, *Simulacra and Simulation,* trans. Sheila F. Glaser (Ann Arbor: University of Michigan Press, 1995).

17. Burke, *Language as Symbolic Action,* 16.

Index

CPSIA information can be obtained at www.ICGtesting.com
Printed in the USA
BVOW05*1720270316

441725BV00002B/2/P